PASSIVE INCOME

USING

AI

Turn algorithms into assets: build real passive income streams with the power of AI.

Written by
Eric LeBouthillier

AcraSolution | 2025 1st Edition
www.acrasolution.com

Preface

Who This Book Is For

This book is written for anyone ready to unlock the financial opportunities created by artificial intelligence. It is ideal for entrepreneurs and small business owners who want to automate revenue streams and scale their businesses without adding more work hours. Freelancers and side hustlers will find strategies to build digital assets that generate money around the clock, while investors and technology enthusiasts will discover how AI is reshaping finance, e-commerce, and online business models. Even complete beginners with no technical background can follow along thanks to clear explanations and step-by-step guidance, while experienced professionals will learn how to future-proof their skills and stay ahead in the fast-changing AI economy.

What You Can Expect

Inside, you can expect a practical roadmap to building real passive income using today's most powerful AI tools. The book starts with the foundations of passive income, separating myths from reality and explaining why artificial intelligence changes the rules. It introduces the most effective platforms and technologies, including chatbots, content generators, trading bots, and e-commerce automation systems. Step-by-step methods show you how to create scalable income streams through digital products, affiliate marketing, and other AI-driven models. Real-world examples and case studies illustrate what works and what doesn't, while dedicated sections address risks, legal considerations, and ethical concerns to keep your journey safe. Finally, you'll explore the future of AI in business and how early adopters can position themselves for long-term financial independence.

Table of Contents

CHAPTER 1

The New Era of Passive Income

How AI Changed the Rules of Wealth Creation

The old rules of wealth creation are crumbling. The model that told you to trade time for money, slowly build capital, and eventually invest in assets—was built for a different era. Artificial Intelligence has fundamentally altered this equation, and the shift isn't coming. It's already here.

Whether you're a solopreneur, a side hustler, or a small business owner, understanding how AI changes the game isn't optional—it's the new price of entry. If you're still thinking of AI as a buzzword or just a tool for tech companies, you're missing the forest for the trees. AI isn't just another app—it's a new economic engine.

The doors it has opened are not just for the ultra-technical or venture-backed. Anyone with access to the internet now has the opportunity to build income-generating systems at a speed and scale that would have been unthinkable even five years ago. But to do that, you have to stop playing by outdated rules.

From Labor-Driven to Leverage-Driven

In the traditional economy, your income ceiling was dictated by your time, effort, and in many cases, your location. To scale, you needed to hire, produce, and manage. That meant overhead, logistics, and risk.

AI changes this by introducing *digital leverage*. You can now build tools, services, and content once—and let them work for you 24/7 with minimal maintenance. AI becomes the labor, the assistant, the analyst, and the distribution channel. Your job shifts from doing the work to designing the system.

Digital leverage is not new. The internet gave us early glimpses—blogs, courses, apps. But until AI, creating something valuable still required significant technical or creative skill. Now, you can rapidly prototype, test, and deploy income-generating assets using plain language prompts and smart workflows.

This is no longer about building the next unicorn startup. It's about creating micro-assets that stack—ebooks, digital tools, affiliate funnels, subscription services, automated agencies—each powered in part or entirely by AI.

Attention Becomes Currency—At Scale

AI doesn't just automate work. It reshapes distribution. With AI-driven content generation, you can create optimized messaging, analyze performance in real time, and adapt instantly—at scale. This means small creators can punch far above their weight class, dominating niche markets with precision messaging.

Attention, not just capital, becomes your leverage. With AI helping you capture and retain audience focus, you build digital trust rapidly. Trust, in turn, converts to influence and sales—whether you're monetizing via products, referrals, licensing, or subscriptions.

The key difference? You're no longer trading time for reach. AI amplifies your signal while reducing your workload. This shift unlocks compounding returns for even the smallest ventures.

The Rise of AI-Native Assets

Traditional passive income streams—rental properties, dividend stocks, royalties—require upfront capital, contracts, and years of patience. AI introduces a new category: *AI-native assets*.

These are income streams that exist entirely in the digital ecosystem, often built with little to no capital. Examples include:

- Auto-updating content hubs that drive affiliate sales
- Prompt-engineered chatbots that offer paid consultations
- AI-designed print-on-demand product lines
- Code-free SaaS tools solving niche problems
- Micro-agencies with automated backends

These assets are not just digital; they are *self-improving*. With well-designed feedback loops, they learn what works and evolve—making them closer to living systems than static products.

The more you iterate, the more accurate, efficient, and profitable they become. AI doesn't just help you build income streams. It helps you refine and multiply them.

Skill Is Still Required—But It's Different Now

Here's where many get it wrong: AI doesn't eliminate the need for skill. It changes *what skill matters*. You no longer need to be a top-tier coder or designer. But you *do* need to understand prompt engineering, data flow, user intent, and digital strategy.

Think of AI as a power tool. In the hands of someone with no blueprint, it just spins. But in the hands of someone with vision, it builds empires. The new skillset is synthesis—knowing how to combine tools, data, and audience insight into systems that deliver value without constant supervision.

This is a massive mindset shift. Instead of asking, *What can I do with AI?*, the real question becomes, *What income-producing system can I build with AI and launch today, that compounds tomorrow?*

The New Timeline of Wealth

Perhaps the most radical shift AI brings to passive income is the timeline. What used to take years to build and test can now be launched in days. The idea-to-income cycle has collapsed.

For example:

- You can go from concept to validated digital product in 48 hours.
- You can launch an AI-driven newsletter and monetize it before your first 500 subscribers.
- You can create a suite of tools that solve micro-problems and license them with zero employees.

These aren't just possibilities. They're already happening. And those who move first—not just fast—are seeing returns exponentially higher than those clinging to legacy methods.

This doesn't mean every AI income idea works. But it does mean the cost of trying has dropped so low, there's no excuse not to build.

Real-World Example: How One Consultant Created a $50K Side Stream with AI

What Happened

In early 2024, a freelance business consultant named Daniel built a simple chatbot using OpenAI and Zapier. It offered automated onboarding audits for small service businesses—basic questions, a scored assessment, and a follow-up PDF with customized advice.

He embedded it on a simple landing page, drove traffic via LinkedIn and YouTube shorts, and offered a paid premium version for $49/month that included templated SOPs and automated email flows.

What Went Right

Daniel didn't overbuild. He identified one painful bottleneck his clients had—onboarding—and automated it using no-code AI tools. He charged a low subscription, kept his promise tight, and used feedback to refine the tool each month.

The result? Within four months, it was making over $4,000/month. No team. No support tickets. And every improvement made the system more valuable.

What We Learn From It

Daniel didn't invent AI. He didn't build an app from scratch. He simply spotted a business problem, used AI to solve it at scale, and priced it like a utility. His real skill wasn't technical—it was in knowing *what to automate*, *who to serve*, and *how to price it*.

This is the core of modern AI-driven passive income: low-code, high-leverage execution.

Common Pitfalls to Avoid

- **Overengineering**: Building overly complex systems before validating the problem or demand.
- **Chasing Trends**: Copying popular AI tools without understanding the business case.
- **No Distribution Plan**: Believing "if you build it, they will come" still works in 2025.
- **Forgetting the Human**: AI may run the backend, but trust, clarity, and value still drive conversions.

Tactical Best Practices

- **Start with Pain**: Identify repeatable business or consumer pain points. AI works best when applied to high-friction processes.
- **Use Low-Code Tools**: Platforms like Zapier, Make, Glide, and ChatGPT APIs let you build income streams without engineering help.
- **Design for Reuse**: Build assets that don't require your constant input—autoresponders, templates, workflows, content calendars.
- **Charge Early**: Monetize fast. Free tools rarely lead to real income. Create tiers or upsells from day one.
- **Iterate Publicly**: Share builds, get feedback, and refine in real time. Transparency builds trust and accelerates product-market fit.

Checklist-Style Action Steps

- Identify 1–2 repetitive problems you or your clients face
- List AI tools or automations that could replace manual work
- Sketch a system (input → AI process → output)
- Choose a low-code platform to test the flow
- Build a landing page explaining the outcome, not the tech
- Price it as a utility, not a feature
- Launch within 7 days, even if imperfect
- Gather feedback, improve weekly, and stack new assets

The world has changed. Building wealth no longer requires gatekeepers, investors, or a full-time grind. But it *does* require a shift in how you see your time, your tools, and your opportunities.

We're not at the beginning of the AI revolution. We're past it. The window is wide open right now—but it won't be forever.

Passive vs Semi-Passive Income Realities

The promise of "make money while you sleep" has always been seductive. But in the AI-driven economy, it's also dangerously misunderstood. Many chase so-called passive income only to find themselves trapped in maintenance-heavy projects or burned out by endless optimization.

To build real income systems—whether passive or semi-passive—you need to understand the difference between myth and reality. This isn't about dreaming. It's about designing income streams that match your time, energy, and goals.

Why Most "Passive Income" Is a Lie

The phrase *passive income* implies total detachment: build it once, forget it forever, and enjoy a continuous cash flow. But in truth, very few income streams are 100% passive. Even rental property requires management. Even dividend investing requires capital and portfolio oversight.

AI tools can *reduce* the time and effort required—but they do not eliminate the need for strategic input, occasional maintenance, or ongoing market awareness.

Most AI-powered income streams fall into the category of *semi-passive*. That means:

- They require upfront effort (design, testing, launching)
- They need occasional updates or refinements
- They benefit from user feedback, growth tactics, and performance reviews

But compared to traditional business models, the leverage is enormous. One weekend of work can generate months—or years—of value, with only light-touch intervention.

The goal isn't to avoid work. It's to **front-load smart work** and build systems that reduce time and dependency without sacrificing revenue.

Understanding the Income Spectrum

Let's break it down clearly:

Type	Description	AI Role	Maintenance Required
Active Income	You trade time for money (freelancing, consulting)	Minimal to none	Ongoing
Semi-Passive Income	Systems that run mostly on their own, with check-ins	Medium to high	Monthly or as-needed
Passive Income	Assets that produce income with almost no input	High automation & autonomy	Quarterly or less

AI enables more income streams to move *left to right* on this spectrum. But the critical question is: **What's the right blend for your goals?**

You may start with semi-passive and optimize toward full automation. Or you may build a portfolio—some assets needing light engagement, others nearly hands-off.

Where AI Truly Excels: Semi-Passive Income

The sweet spot for AI income today is **semi-passive systems with high ROI and minimal complexity**. These include:

- **AI-curated newsletters** that pull insights from industry feeds and send weekly summaries to subscribers
- **Niche content hubs** that update automatically and monetize through affiliate links
- **Prompt-based micro-tools** (e.g., legal clause generators, email optimizers) with usage-based pricing
- **Low-touch digital products** like templates, scripts, or Notion dashboards enhanced with AI functionality

These systems require:

- Strategic thinking up front
- Minimal but regular performance tuning
- Occasional upgrades to remain relevant

But they offer something crucial: **asymmetrical returns**. Once created, they can earn indefinitely—without trading hours for dollars.

Real-World Example: Scaling Semi-Passive Success With AI

What Happened

Lina, a copywriter and content strategist, wanted to escape the active-income trap of project-based freelancing. She identified a need: small ecommerce brands struggling with email copywriting.

She used AI to create a set of smart email templates—pre-prompted Google Docs powered by ChatGPT API. She packaged them into a downloadable toolkit with a short tutorial video and sold it for $79.

She launched via her email list, LinkedIn posts, and a few targeted Reddit threads. In the first month: $2,800. In the second month, with minor tweaks: $6,100.

What Went Right

Lina built once, distributed widely, and responded to feedback. She spent 2–3 hours per week answering emails, improving prompts, and testing new audiences.

Her AI asset didn't run entirely on autopilot—but it worked far more efficiently than her freelance gigs. She converted expertise into a scalable product, and AI handled the customization.

What We Learn From It

This was semi-passive done right. Lina:

- Solved a clear pain point
- Used AI to scale her core skill
- Automated delivery and fulfillment
- Built a lightweight support system
- Let her audience guide future versions

She didn't aim for perfection. She aimed for velocity—and upgraded only what the market proved was valuable.

Common Mistakes That Kill Passive Income Potential

- **Trying to skip the validation phase**: If no one wants your product, automating it won't help.
- **Ignoring updates and optimization**: Even the best tools go stale if left untouched.
- **Over-dependence on a single platform**: Relying entirely on one AI tool, traffic source, or monetization channel creates vulnerability.
- **Automating too early**: Don't optimize what hasn't earned. Manual first, then automate.
- **Mistaking "AI-powered" for "AI-reliable"**: AI can create, but *you* must ensure it delivers actual value.

Tactical Best Practices

- **Start with semi-passive in mind**: Build lean. Launch early. Automate only what works.
- **Bundle your skills**: Don't just sell information—add prompts, tools, or workflows that speed results.
- **Price for outcomes**: People pay for results, not tools. Frame your AI product around what it *does* for them.
- **Build in layers**: Start with one product. Add upsells, subscriptions, or bundled offers once it's proven.
- **Set a review cadence**: Monthly check-ins to test, improve, or optimize are enough for most AI systems.

Checklist-Style Action Steps

- List your current active income sources
- Identify which parts of your workflow are repeatable
- Select one to turn into a semi-passive offer (product, template, or tool)
- Use AI to enhance creation speed or value
- Build a distribution plan with 1–2 simple channels (email, YouTube, Twitter, etc.)
- Track performance weekly, review monthly
- Apply feedback before automating further
- Stack your next asset only after the first earns

How to Spot a Real Passive Income Opportunity

Ask yourself:

- Can this generate value *without* me being involved day-to-day?
- Is there clear, recurring demand for the outcome it delivers?
- Can it be built and tested in under 30 days?
- Can AI reduce or replace at least 50% of the manual work?
- If I had to shut off ads, platforms, or my time—would the system still earn?

If you answer "yes" to at least four, you're looking at a viable semi-passive model—with the potential to grow into true passive income over time.

The AI era doesn't promise freedom from work—it offers *freedom through smarter work*. The systems you build now become income infrastructure tomorrow.

The Automation Advantage: Scale Without Staff

Hiring used to be the only way to scale. If you wanted to grow, you added people. More clients meant more project managers. More sales meant more reps. More complexity meant more operations. But with the rise of AI automation, that equation no longer holds.

Today, you can scale processes, revenue, and reach—not by growing a team, but by deploying systems. AI automation doesn't just replace tasks—it rewrites the logic of scale itself. What once required full departments can now be executed by solo operators using a tightly integrated toolset.

This changes everything for the modern entrepreneur. No payroll. No HR headaches. No complex org charts. Just lean, high-output systems that run at scale—with minimal overhead.

Scaling Isn't About More Work—It's About Less You

Traditional growth assumes effort scales linearly: more clients equals more work. But automation breaks this pattern. It allows your systems to handle the *next 100 customers* with the same effort as the last 10.

That's because AI and no-code platforms let you:

- Automate lead qualification and onboarding
- Deliver content or products instantly, without fulfillment delays
- Respond to FAQs and customer issues via chatbots
- Generate reports, proposals, or custom outputs on demand
- Personalize communication without lifting a finger

These aren't hypothetical. They're running today—in small businesses, solo consultancies, even side hustles.

The secret? System design. Not just automating *tasks*, but *outcomes*. That's how you grow without hiring.

The Five Layers of an AI-Automated Business

A fully automated AI income stream typically includes five functional layers. Mastering these lets you build a business that scales without staff.

1. **Input Capture**
   - Forms, quizzes, chatbots, or lead magnets that collect data from users.
   - Example: An AI-powered intake form that routes leads based on needs.
2. **Processing Logic**
   - AI models or automation flows that process input into value.
   - Example: A prompt that turns client pain points into a marketing plan.
3. **Output Delivery**
   - Automatic generation and sending of the deliverable or result.
   - Example: An automated PDF guide customized to each user's business.

4. **Follow-Up & Retention**
   - Email sequences, SMS updates, retargeting, or loyalty campaigns.
   - Example: A Zapier flow that sends a weekly AI tip tailored to user actions.
5. **Optimization & Feedback**
   - Analytics dashboards and AI-assisted reviews to improve performance.
   - Example: Tools like Pendo or Segment that track behavior and adjust offers.

AI AUTOMATION LAYERS IN A SOLO-RUN BUSINESS

INPUT

|

PROCESSING

|

OUTPUT

|

FOLLOW-UP

|

FEEDBACK OPTIMIZATION

This layered model replaces traditional functions like sales, operations, support, and customer success. Instead of managing people, you manage flows and prompts.

Real-World Example: Scaling a Coaching Offer Without a Team

What Happened

Rachel, a productivity coach, wanted to stop trading time for Zoom calls. She took her most requested service—a 90-minute systems audit—and converted it into a self-service AI experience.

She created:

- A dynamic intake form that mapped user behaviors
- An AI prompt engine that generated a custom notion workspace
- An automated video walkthrough tailored to the audit results
- A follow-up email flow with optional upsells and ongoing coaching support

All of this ran through Zapier, Typeform, OpenAI API, and Loom.

What Went Right

Rachel used to do four of these audits per week at $350 each. After building the automated system, she sold the same outcome for $149—and sold 80 in her first 30 days.

She added a premium coaching upgrade for $500, which converted 12% of users.

Zero employees. Zero delivery time. Just system refinement.

What We Learn From It

Rachel scaled *outcome delivery*, not labor. She built around the customer transformation, not her own time. The AI system did 90% of the work. She showed up only where her insight was truly needed.

This is the core of automation: not removing humans entirely, but *removing humans where they don't add value.*

Common Pitfalls That Block Automation Success

- **Automating the wrong things**: If your offer isn't validated, automation will only scale failure.
- **Overcomplication**: Too many tools, too much logic, not enough clarity.
- **No human fallback**: AI can handle 90%, but customers need an escape hatch for support or escalation.
- **Ignoring UX**: Automation must feel seamless and human— not clunky or robotic.
- **Forgetting updates**: AI flows require occasional tuning. Set reminders to review quarterly.

Tactical Best Practices

- **Start with what repeats**: Identify any task you do more than three times a week. Automate that first.
- **Use modular tools**: Tools like Make, Zapier, Airtable, Notion, and OpenAI are flexible and future-proof.
- **Build micro-flows**: Don't automate your whole business at once. Create small, repeatable wins.
- **Test every automation live**: Run through your own system like a customer. Watch for friction.
- **Log and track**: Use tools like Slack notifications or simple dashboards to monitor what's running and where it breaks.

Checklist-Style Action Steps

- List your top 3 most repeated tasks (sales, content, fulfillment, etc.)
- Map the customer journey from lead to delivery
- Identify where AI or automation could reduce your time by 50%+
- Choose one process to automate end-to-end
- Build a v1 with low-code tools (Zapier, ChatGPT API, Airtable, etc.)
- Test with 5–10 users, collect feedback, refine
- Set a monthly system review schedule
- Document every automation for backup or handoff

How to Think Like a System Builder

If you want to scale without staff, your mindset must shift from *doing* to *designing*.

Ask:

- Where am I repeating myself unnecessarily?
- What information am I collecting manually that AI can interpret?
- What decisions am I making that could be logic-based?
- How can I turn my service into a *flow* instead of a meeting?

Design once. Deploy forever. Update occasionally.

That's the new growth playbook—and it doesn't require an org chart, a payroll system, or investor funding. Just clarity, strategy, and the right tools.

Risks of "AI Hype" vs. Sustainable Strategies

The AI gold rush is in full swing—and with it, a flood of noise, misinformation, and get-rich-quick schemes. Scroll through any business forum, YouTube channel, or LinkedIn thread, and you'll find bold promises: "Earn $10,000 a week with this ChatGPT trick," or "Automate your entire business in 48 hours." But behind the flashy headlines lies a harsh truth: **most of what's being sold under the banner of AI income is unstable, short-lived, and deeply unsustainable.**

If you're serious about building income streams that *last*—not just spike—then you need to see past the hype and focus on strategic, reality-based use of AI. This section will show you what to avoid, what to build, and how to separate trends from tactics that stand the test of time.

Hype Is Fast Money with a Short Shelf Life

Many AI business models you see online today fall into one of three traps:

1. **Platform Dependency**
   Example: Selling low-effort AI-generated books, logos, or designs on Fiverr or Etsy. These are easy to copy, and platforms quickly penalize repetition or low-value content.
2. **Prompt Chaining Gimmicks**
   Example: Selling "secret prompts" or reselling ChatGPT outputs as full services. These lack defensibility, can be replicated by anyone, and provide little real customer value.
3. **Zero-Differentiation Clones**
   Example: "I made $5K selling an AI planner, now you can too." Once a tactic becomes public, competition floods in. Without a brand, audience, or unique angle, you're invisible.

What all of these have in common is *fragility*. They depend on trends, loopholes, and temporary arbitrage—not on value creation, customer relationships, or long-term leverage.

If your business only works because no one else knows about it yet, it won't last. True AI-powered wealth comes from building *systems*, *assets*, and *trust*—not from chasing hacks.

What Sustainable Looks Like in an AI-Powered Business

A sustainable strategy does not mean slow or conservative. It means **durable**—something that holds up under pressure, adapts over time, and grows in value the more it runs.

Here's what defines sustainability in AI income:

- **Real Problem Solving**: You're addressing a pain point that matters—something people would pay for even *without* AI involved.
- **AI as an Enhancer, Not the Product**: The value is in the outcome, not in the fact that it's AI-powered.
- **Own Your Distribution**: You're not relying 100% on someone else's platform for traffic, leads, or reach.
- **Simple, Documented Systems**: You've built processes you understand, can improve, and can hand off.
- **Consistent Value Delivery**: Your AI doesn't just work once—it delivers repeatable, reliable output with minimal errors or friction.

In short: *sustainable businesses solve problems in ways that scale, improve, and compound.*

Real-World Example: The Difference Between Hype and Strategy

What Happened

In late 2023, two entrepreneurs launched AI-powered product businesses.

- Jake built a Shopify store selling AI-generated T-shirt slogans. He used Midjourney and ChatGPT to spin out hundreds of designs and loaded them into a print-on-demand system. His TikToks went viral. He made $18,000 in his first two weeks.
- Maya built a B2B lead qualification system using OpenAI, Airtable, and Zapier. Her system helped niche SaaS companies qualify inbound leads by scoring form responses and routing them to sales teams. She charged a monthly subscription and offered light customization.

By month four, Jake's store was banned by his print provider for spammy content. His traffic dried up. Sales vanished.

Meanwhile, Maya's system had 14 clients on $297/month retainers—and her churn was near zero.

What Went Right—and Wrong

Jake chased virality. He had no brand, no customer insight, and no defensibility. Maya solved a painful problem, built systems instead of hacks, and created predictable value.

The lesson is simple: **short-term gains from hype are unreliable. But well-designed, AI-enhanced systems create compounding income and trust.**

Common Pitfalls in the AI Hustle Culture

- **Over-reliance on automation**: Automating junk still produces junk. If the core offer isn't strong, automation only scales the weakness.
- **Chasing novelty over value**: Being "first" doesn't matter if the product doesn't solve a real problem or sustain user interest.
- **Ignoring customer experience**: AI doesn't excuse poor design, confusing flows, or vague promises. Users still expect clarity, support, and trust.
- **No feedback loops**: Without a way to gather and respond to user input, your system will rot over time.
- **Scalability without support**: Going viral with no infrastructure in place leads to broken systems, lost reputation, and burnout.

Tactical Best Practices

- **Anchor everything in user need**: Start with a problem that causes friction, delay, or confusion. Build AI around that pain—not just around what's trendy.
- **Test manually before automating**: Deliver the value yourself a few times to understand the nuance, then let AI take over the repeatable parts.
- **Build assets, not tricks**: Templates, systems, calculators, reports—things people can use repeatedly—will outperform content farms and gimmicks every time.
- **Track value, not just volume**: Pay attention to retention, testimonials, and referrals—not just one-time sales or clicks.
- **Use AI to enhance your advantage**: Whether you're a designer, analyst, coach, or consultant—let AI extend your strengths, not replace them.

Checklist-Style Action Steps

- Audit your current or planned AI product: Is it solving a specific pain point?
- List the top 3 risks to its long-term survival (platform rules, competition, content decay)
- Define what your *unfair advantage* is (skill, audience, insight, niche positioning)
- Document the core value flow of your system (input → processing → output → feedback)
- Identify one area you're chasing trend over substance— refactor it
- Add at least one data or feedback loop (form, survey, usage data, reviews)
- Set a quarterly system review: update prompts, check automation health, optimize outcomes

The Litmus Test: Is This Hype or Strategy?

Ask yourself:

- Would this business still work if AI became mainstream and commoditized tomorrow?
- Am I solving something painful, or just interesting?
- Can I explain the value without saying "AI" even once?
- Is this something I would use and pay for myself?
- Do I have a long-term reason to keep improving this?

If you answer "no" to any of these, you may be riding a hype wave instead of building something that lasts.

There's nothing wrong with short-term wins. But don't confuse momentum with durability. If your goal is financial freedom, flexibility, and long-term control, you need to build *systems, not stunts*.

CHAPTER 2

The AI Toolbox You Need

Core AI Platforms (Text, Image, Video, Code, Voice)

To build sustainable, semi-passive income streams with AI, you need more than hype—you need the right tools. The AI landscape is vast, but most income-generating systems rely on five functional domains: **text, image, video, code, and voice**.

Understanding how to choose and apply the right platforms in each category is critical. Each has strengths, limitations, and ideal use cases. When layered strategically, they give you full-stack capability without writing a single line of code or hiring a team.

This section will give you the curated, business-ready overview of the top platforms in each AI domain—and how to apply them to real income-generating systems.

TEXT: Your Engine for Content, Copy, and Knowledge Work

Text-based AI is the most mature and widely accessible category. It powers everything from blog posts to customer support chatbots to product descriptions—and it's often the starting point for solo entrepreneurs building AI income streams.

Core Use Cases:

- Content creation (articles, emails, newsletters, social posts)
- Copywriting (landing pages, ads, CTAs, funnels)
- Chatbots and conversational flows
- Lead magnets, ebooks, and templates
- Report generation and summarization
- Prompt-based workflows (e.g., content audit tools, brief builders)

Top Platforms:

- **OpenAI (ChatGPT / GPT-4)**: Industry leader in natural language generation and understanding. Ideal for writing, reasoning, and contextual outputs.
- **Claude by Anthropic**: Strong contextual comprehension, long-memory use cases, and safety alignment.
- **Jasper AI**: Tailored for marketers, with brand voice tools and templates.
- **Copy.ai**: Prebuilt workflows for startups, sales, and marketing.
- **Writer.com**: Designed for enterprise and team-based use, with brand governance features.

Best Practice Insight:
Don't just use text AI to generate content—use it to systematize insight. Create prompt-based workflows where users input a few variables and receive a tailored outcome (audit, checklist, plan, summary). These are income-generating tools, not just content toys.

IMAGE: Visual Output That Scales Design Without Designers

Image generation has evolved rapidly. You can now produce custom product visuals, marketing graphics, thumbnails, or even brand assets on demand. This creates major leverage for creators, ecommerce businesses, and solopreneurs.

Core Use Cases:

- Product mockups and branded visuals
- Print-on-demand (T-shirts, mugs, posters)
- Thumbnails and social graphics
- Illustration and cover design
- UI/UX concept drafts and storyboards

Top Platforms:

- **Midjourney**: Known for aesthetic quality, ideal for creative work and stylized visuals.
- **DALL·E (OpenAI)**: Integrated into ChatGPT; strong for functional images and variations.
- **Leonardo.ai**: Focused on game assets, design packs, and e-commerce visuals.
- **Adobe Firefly**: Useful for Photoshop-native users and brand-safe content.
- **Canva + AI tools**: Not a generator, but offers AI-accelerated image creation and enhancement tools.

Best Practice Insight:
Image AI becomes powerful when tied to utility. For example, generating hundreds of niche designs for a print-on-demand store or creating dynamic visuals for a content automation funnel.

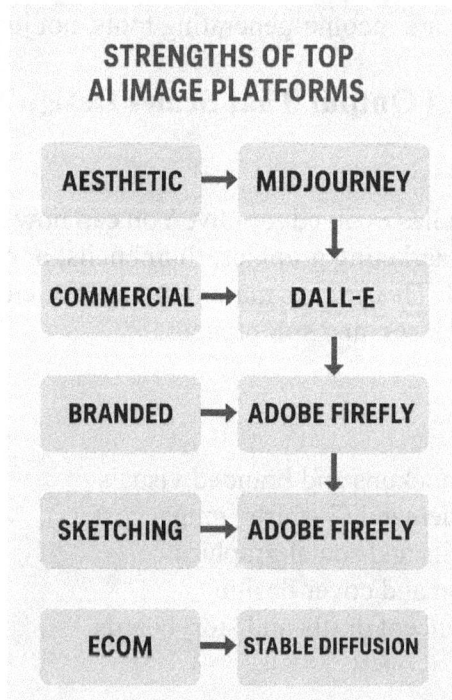

**STRENGTHS OF TOP
AI IMAGE PLATFORMS**

AESTHETIC → MIDJOURNEY

↓

COMMERCIAL → DALL-E

↓

BRANDED → ADOBE FIREFLY

↓

SKETCHING → ADOBE FIREFLY

ECOM → STABLE DIFFUSION

VIDEO: Rapid Creation for High-Engagement Assets

Video is the most attention-rich format online—and AI is making it easier than ever to generate explainer videos, faceless YouTube content, product walkthroughs, and marketing assets *without filming anything*.

Core Use Cases:

- YouTube channel creation (faceless, automated scripts)
- Tutorial and course creation
- Video ads and landing page explainers
- Text-to-video content repurposing
- Avatar-led coaching or spokesperson videos

Top Platforms:

- **Pictory.ai**: Turns text or blog content into animated videos with voiceovers and stock footage.
- **Synthesia**: Create human-like avatars that deliver your scripts in multiple languages.
- **RunwayML**: Advanced video editing, generation, and AI inpainting.
- **Lumen5**: Converts articles or scripts into social media–friendly video content.
- **HeyGen**: Similar to Synthesia, strong in avatar generation and multilingual use cases.

Best Practice Insight:
Automate short-form content at scale. Combine ChatGPT for scriptwriting, Pictory for video creation, and Hootsuite or Buffer for scheduled posting. This creates a high-output content engine with minimal time investment.

CODE: Build Tools Without Developers

You don't need to write code to build code. With AI code generation, you can create micro-tools, web apps, automations, and even SaaS MVPs—without hiring developers. This is especially powerful when paired with no-code platforms.

Core Use Cases:

- Chrome extensions and micro-apps
- SaaS product prototypes
- Website backends and logic
- Custom automations and data parsing
- Prompt-powered internal tools

Top Platforms:

- **GitHub Copilot**: Best for developers using VSCode— suggests full code blocks and integrations.
- **OpenAI Code Interpreter (a.k.a. Advanced Data Analysis)**: Ideal for logic-heavy prompts, calculations, and data tasks.
- **Replit**: Full in-browser coding with AI co-pilot for instant deployment.
- **Bubble + AI plugins**: Build full apps with drag-and-drop and embed GPT-powered logic.
- **Zapier + Code by Zapier**: Light logic and task automation via snippets.

Best Practice Insight:
Build niche solutions, not general ones. AI code tools let you create hyper-targeted utilities (e.g., "Amazon listing title optimizer for handmade jewelry") that solve specific business pains and can be sold, licensed, or gated via subscription.

VOICE: Spoken AI That Sells, Supports, and Teaches

AI-generated voice is no longer robotic—it's conversational, multilingual, and adaptive. Voice tools now power podcasts, onboarding flows, customer support systems, and even AI sales agents.

Core Use Cases:

- Audiobooks and podcast narration
- Customer service and call center agents
- Course voiceovers and training content
- Multilingual product localization
- Smart IVR (interactive voice response) flows

Top Platforms:

- **ElevenLabs**: Industry leader in realistic voice synthesis with emotion control.
- **Descript**: Great for podcast editing, voice cloning, and multi-format exports.
- **WellSaid Labs**: Enterprise-grade voiceover with studio-quality output.
- **Speechify**: Ideal for turning text into narrated content quickly.
- **Replica Studios**: Targeted at game development and emotional voice acting.

Best Practice Insight:
Voice AI works best when it connects to a system. For example, you could combine ElevenLabs with an AI script generator to create an end-to-end podcast engine—or use it to narrate personalized onboarding flows for your SaaS or service.

Platform Layering: Combine, Don't Just Consume

The real power of these platforms is not in isolation—but in **combination**. When layered into a workflow, they create fully automated or semi-passive income machines.

Example Stack: AI-Powered Lead Magnet Funnel

1. **Text AI** (ChatGPT): Generate a personalized checklist or strategy plan.
2. **Image AI** (Midjourney): Create branded cover visuals or illustrations.
3. **Video AI** (Pictory): Turn the plan into a narrated walkthrough.
4. **Voice AI** (ElevenLabs): Use natural voiceovers instead of robotic narration.
5. **Automation (Zapier + Notion)**: Deliver the final package instantly after opt-in.

Each layer builds value, trust, and perceived quality—without increasing workload.

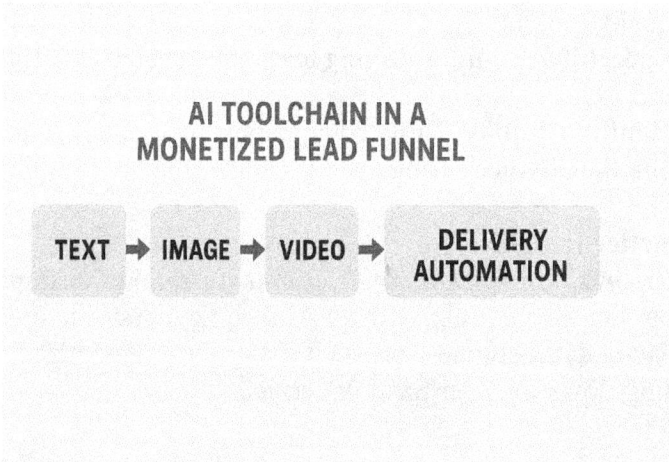

AI TOOLCHAIN IN A MONETIZED LEAD FUNNEL

TEXT ➡ IMAGE ➡ VIDEO ➡ DELIVERY AUTOMATION

Checklist-Style Action Steps

- Choose one income idea (product, service, tool) and define the required outputs (text, image, video, etc.)
- Identify which AI tools can cover each output without manual effort
- Test each platform in isolation to understand output quality and limits
- Design a workflow connecting at least 3 tools (e.g., text → image → delivery)
- Track time saved and output consistency—refine where quality drops
- Document your AI stack for repeatability and potential handoff
- Begin building your first end-to-end AI system—optimize weekly

No-Code + API Integration for Non-Technical Founders

One of the most powerful shifts in the AI era isn't just the technology itself—it's the fact that you no longer need to be technical to *build with it*. Thanks to the rise of no-code platforms and plug-and-play API integrations, non-technical founders can now create sophisticated systems that were once only possible with full-stack engineering teams.

This changes the playing field completely. If you have an idea, a clear audience, and a real solution, you can now build and launch a fully automated income-generating product—*without writing a single line of code*.

In this section, we'll break down exactly how non-technical founders can combine no-code platforms with AI APIs to create lean, scalable, and maintainable business systems.

What Is No-Code and Why It Matters

No-code tools let you build apps, workflows, websites, automations, and databases through visual interfaces instead of programming languages. These platforms abstract away the complexity, letting you focus on logic, user experience, and outcomes—not syntax.

For founders, this means:

- Faster prototyping (days, not months)
- Lower cost (no need to hire developers early)
- Full control over iteration, testing, and updates
- Easy integration with AI models via API or built-in plugins

No-code isn't about avoiding tech. It's about *accelerating execution* by turning ideas into systems—without technical bottlenecks.

The Core No-Code Stack

There are dozens of tools, but most AI-powered income systems can be built with a modular stack of five core functions:

Function	Tool Examples	Purpose
Frontend (UI)	Softr, Glide, Typedream	Build client-facing websites, dashboards, or interfaces
Backend Logic	Zapier, Make (Integromat), Pabbly	Connect tools, run automations, handle logic and triggers
Data Storage	Airtable, Google Sheets, Notion	Store inputs, variables, outputs, and logs
AI Integration	OpenAI, ElevenLabs, Stability API	Plug in language, image, voice models for dynamic output
Payment + Auth	Stripe, Gumroad, Outseta, Memberstack	Handle subscriptions, paywalls, and user authentication

These tools speak to each other via **APIs**—a standardized way for software to send and receive data. No need to code APIs yourself. Most no-code platforms let you connect via a simple visual builder, webhook, or integration library.

Real-World Example: Creating a Passive AI Audit Tool Without Code

What Happened

Sam, a solopreneur with no technical background, built a niche "AI for podcasters" onboarding tool. Users filled out a short form about their show goals, audience, and format. In return, they received a personalized PDF with:

- Episode topic suggestions
- Hook and title templates
- Monetization strategy based on their niche

Sam built it using:

- **Typeform** for the front-end form
- **Airtable** to store inputs and trigger workflows
- **OpenAI API via Make.com** to generate the custom content
- **PDF.co** to format and generate a branded download
- **Stripe** ⏐ **Outseta** to gate access behind a $29 paywall

Time to build: 9 days.
Ongoing time required: <2 hours/month.
Monthly revenue after 3 months: ~$1,700
Growth: Organic referrals + SEO blog posts written by ChatGPT.

What We Learn From It

Sam didn't invent a new technology. He *combined* no-code tools with smart AI prompts to solve a very specific problem. He didn't need a dev team—just clarity of purpose, a little patience, and access to tutorials and documentation.

Key Integrations Every Founder Should Know

You don't need to master them all, but these foundational integrations give you incredible leverage:

- **OpenAI + Zapier**
  Trigger GPT-4 to generate copy, responses, summaries, or plans based on user input.
- **Airtable + Make**
  Use Airtable as your logic center (like a database) and Make to automate branching logic or API calls.
- **Webhooks + ChatGPT API**
  Connect any tool with webhook support (e.g., Typeform, Calendly) to AI-driven responses in real time.
- **Stripe + Outseta**
  Accept payments, manage memberships, and lock AI tools behind authentication—no code required.
- **Google Sheets + OpenAI**
  Auto-fill content, insights, and suggestions based on spreadsheet data (great for content ops or pricing engines).

Common Mistakes Non-Technical Builders Should Avoid

- **Trying to build everything at once**: Start with one clear asset or use case. Simplicity wins early.
- **Not testing workflows manually**: Always walk through your system like a user before letting others in.
- **Skipping documentation**: As your system grows, you'll forget how you built it. Document every step.
- **Forgetting fail-safes**: Build in fallback conditions (e.g., "If GPT fails, send alert").
- **Relying on free-tier limits**: Always check rate limits, API costs, and tool caps before scaling up.

Tactical Best Practices

- **Map before building**: Sketch your workflow (input → process → output) before touching any tool.
- **Use templates**: Most no-code tools offer ready-made templates—customize instead of building from scratch.
- **Name variables clearly**: You'll use them across tools. Clean naming saves hours later.
- **Test APIs with Postman or webhook.site**: This helps debug early without frustration.
- **Plan for scale**: Use Airtable over Sheets for performance. Add backups or logs for mission-critical automations.

Checklist-Style Action Steps

- Identify a task you do 3+ times/week that involves data or writing
- Sketch a workflow showing where automation and AI could replace manual work
- Choose one frontend tool (Typeform, Softr, etc.) to collect inputs
- Connect that input to Airtable or Google Sheets to store and organize
- Use Zapier or Make to trigger OpenAI API based on inputs
- Deliver the output via email, PDF, or dashboard
- Add payment or access control (if monetized)
- Test, refine, and launch with 5–10 users before scaling

The New Competitive Edge for Founders

In the past, founders needed three things to build digital products: an idea, capital, and a technical cofounder. Today, you just need the idea—and a clear understanding of how to assemble tools.

AI and no-code stacks give you the same firepower as an early startup team. The difference is speed, cost, and ownership. You don't have to wait for someone else to build it. You *can build it yourself*—and iterate as fast as your market responds.

Automation Stacks: Zapier, Make, and Custom Scripts

Building income-generating systems with AI is not just about clever prompts or beautiful interfaces—it's about **glue**. That glue is automation. The ability to move data between tools, trigger AI workflows based on user behavior, and deliver outcomes instantly is what turns a clever idea into a monetizable asset.

Automation stacks are how solo founders, microbusinesses, and side-hustlers achieve *scale without code*. And whether you're using tools like **Zapier**, **Make (formerly Integromat)**, or rolling your own with **custom scripts**, your automation strategy defines how efficient, flexible, and resilient your AI income engine will be.

This section breaks down each type of automation platform—what it's good for, where it falls short, and how to stack them into a workflow that grows with your business.

What Is an Automation Stack?

An automation stack is the system of tools, integrations, and logic flows that power your AI-based income stream. It connects the parts of your system—form inputs, data processing, content generation, delivery, payment, and follow-up—so you don't have to do it manually.

A basic AI income workflow might look like this:

1. **User Input** (e.g., a quiz or form)
2. **Data Capture** (e.g., store answers in Airtable)
3. **AI Processing** (e.g., generate recommendations using OpenAI)
4. **Asset Creation** (e.g., compile into a PDF or email)
5. **Delivery** (e.g., email the user or push to a dashboard)
6. **Follow-up** (e.g., send thank-you email, upsell offer, or retargeting ad)

Without automation, you'd have to do this manually. With the right stack, it runs while you sleep.

Zapier: The Business-Friendly Automation Standard

Best For: Fast builds, broad integrations, minimal setup
Skill Level: Beginner to intermediate
Strengths:

- Massive library of prebuilt integrations
- Very easy to use and widely supported
- Excellent for marketing, ecommerce, forms, CRMs, and email tools

Limitations:

- Less flexible for complex logic or large data sets
- Limited branching and iteration options
- Pricing can scale up quickly with volume

When to Use:

- Quickly connect popular apps (e.g., Typeform → OpenAI → Gmail)
- Automate lead capture, onboarding emails, or payment confirmations
- Trigger AI outputs on form submission or payment events

Real Use Case:
You run a paid Notion template shop. A user buys via Gumroad. Zapier listens for the purchase event, triggers a GPT-generated personalized onboarding guide, and sends it to the customer via Gmail—all in under 30 seconds.

Make (Integromat): The Power Builder's Choice

Best For: Visual mapping, advanced logic, scalable workflows
Skill Level: Intermediate to advanced
Strengths:

- Visual scenario builder makes complex flows easy to manage
- Supports iterators, routers, conditional logic, and error handling
- Better pricing model for high-volume users

Limitations:

- Steeper learning curve than Zapier
- Some tools require manual token/API connection
- Debugging can be more involved

When to Use:

- Automating multi-step, data-driven workflows
- Connecting tools not supported in Zapier
- Handling complex user journeys (e.g., choose-your-path assessments)

Real Use Case:
You run an AI-powered marketing plan generator. A user fills out a detailed form. Make stores their answers, queries GPT-4 for multiple outputs (brand positioning, content strategy, and channel plan), compiles everything into a PDF, stores it in Google Drive, and emails the user a download link—with zero manual input.

Custom Scripts: Maximum Flexibility, Maximum Responsibility

Best For: Full customization, private API handling, edge-case workflows
Skill Level: Advanced (or via technical contractor)
Strengths:

- Unlimited control and logic customization
- Better performance for large-scale or data-heavy tasks
- Ideal for SaaS prototypes or monetized API products

Limitations:

- Requires programming skills (typically Python or JavaScript)
- Higher time cost and maintenance overhead
- Must handle errors, retries, and scaling manually

When to Use:

- Creating monetizable APIs or internal tools
- Handling sensitive data securely
- Scaling beyond the limits of Zapier/Make

Real Use Case:
You create a subscription service that auto-generates LinkedIn content for sales teams. Your Python script pulls user profile data, queries GPT-4 for weekly posts, formats them, schedules via LinkedIn API, and logs performance analytics. It runs on a cron job, fully autonomous—and deeply tailored.

Choosing the Right Tool for Your Stage

Need	Use This Tool
Just getting started	**Zapier**
Need logic and control	**Make**
Building a product/API/tool	**Custom Script**
Scaling a validated service	**Make + Script**
Budget conscious, high volume	**Make**
Familiarity and speed	**Zapier**

Start with **Zapier** for MVPs. Move to **Make** as complexity increases. Use **custom scripts** when your business depends on edge-case logic or full-stack deployment.

Common Mistakes When Building Automation Stacks

- **Automating too early**: Validate manually first. Don't automate something no one wants.
- **Overbuilding**: If your workflow has 40+ steps before you've launched, you're doing too much.
- **Ignoring error handling**: Plan for tool failures, API limits, or missing data.
- **No monitoring**: If something breaks, how will you know? Add logging or alert systems.
- **Poor naming conventions**: Use clear names for variables, steps, and documents—especially in multi-tool flows.

Tactical Best Practices

- **Map your flow before building**: Use whiteboards or tools like Whimsical, Miro, or Lucidchart.
- **Use Make for branching decisions**: Perfect for tiered offers, conditional flows, or multi-output AI systems.
- **Log everything**: Store a copy of each transaction, prompt, output, and error in Airtable or Google Sheets.

- **Test with live users**: Nothing reveals weaknesses like real-world data.
- **Schedule reviews**: Automations rot over time. Set a monthly check-in for each stack.

Checklist-Style Action Steps

- Document your business flow from input to output to follow-up
- Choose your automation tool based on complexity and budget
- Start by building one automated process end-to-end (e.g., lead magnet delivery)
- Add error alerts via email, Slack, or logging
- Track all prompts, outputs, and user interactions in a data sheet
- Create a second automation only *after* the first is running smoothly
- Review and refine automations monthly based on real user feedback

Automate Systems, Not Just Tasks

It's tempting to use automation just to save time on chores. But the real value lies in **building entire income systems that run with minimal human involvement**.

The automation stack you choose should:

- Scale with usage
- Handle complexity as you grow
- Give you control over outcomes, not just outputs

You're not just connecting tools. You're designing an invisible workforce—a virtual operations engine that works on weekends, holidays, and while you sleep.

Choosing the Right Tools Without Subscription Bloat

The appeal of AI and no-code tools is obvious: speed, convenience, and automation at your fingertips. But for many founders, solopreneurs, and small business owners, there's a darker side—**subscription bloat**.

It starts with good intentions: $19/month here for an AI writing assistant, $29/month there for an automation platform, another $15/month for design tools. Suddenly, you're burning $300+ monthly before your first customer has even paid you.

This isn't just a financial problem. It's a strategic one. Every tool you add comes with cognitive load, system complexity, integration risk, and potential failure points.

In the AI-powered passive income landscape, **lean stacks win**. You don't need more tools—you need *the right tools*, chosen with discipline and purpose.

This section will help you choose strategically, consolidate ruthlessly, and build income systems that maximize output—not overhead.

The Real Cost of Tool Overload

Subscription bloat doesn't just drain your wallet. It affects:

- **Profitability**: Every $29/month tool eats into your margins. When you're bootstrapping or testing a new product, that can be the difference between a viable offer and a sunk cost.
- **Clarity**: Juggling 12+ tools creates confusion. You forget which tool does what, where your data lives, and how to fix something when it breaks.

- **Maintenance**: More tools = more updates, more API keys, more points of failure.
- **Focus**: Each tool adds UI, options, dashboards, and distractions. Tool sprawl is the enemy of velocity.

Successful builders know this: **simplicity scales**. The more lean your tech stack, the easier it is to launch, iterate, and grow.

The 80/20 Rule of AI Tool Selection

In most AI income systems, **80% of your results will come from 20% of your tools**. Your goal should be to identify the *critical few* platforms that deliver the most value—and eliminate or defer the rest.

The five essential categories are:

1. **AI Engine** — Text, code, or content generation
   → Example: ChatGPT (OpenAI) or Claude
2. **Frontend/Input** — User interaction (form, page, chatbot)
   → Example: Typeform, Softr, or Tally
3. **Backend/Logic** — Automation and workflow builder
   → Example: Make or Zapier
4. **Storage** — Where inputs, outputs, or logs are stored
   → Example: Airtable or Google Sheets
5. **Delivery** — Where or how the user receives the outcome
   → Example: Email, Notion, PDF generator, or dashboard

If you choose **one tool per function**, you can build nearly any AI-powered business system.

Anything beyond this should be justified by clear ROI or workflow simplicity.

Tool Consolidation Tactics

Before you subscribe to anything new, ask:

- **Do I already have another tool that can do this (even less elegantly)?**
- **Can this task be outsourced to AI or handled manually for now?**
- **Does this tool replace two or more existing ones?**
- **Can I use the free tier for my current stage of growth?**

Below are some smart ways to **combine functions** and cut down subscriptions:

Goal	Overlapping Tools to Consolidate	Recommended Lean Option
Form + automation	Typeform + Zapier	Tally + Make
Email + CRM + funnels	ConvertKit + Mailchimp + Zapier	Outseta or Beehiiv
Website + dashboard	Webflow + Memberstack + Airtable	Softr or Typedream
File delivery + hosting	Google Drive + Dropbox + Gumroad	Notion + Stripe + EmailOctopus
Prompt building + delivery	Jasper + ChatGPT + PDF plugin	ChatGPT + Make + PDF.co

Free-Tier Friendly Tools That Scale With You

If you're just starting out, these platforms offer **generous free tiers** that support real use cases—not just toy projects.

- **OpenAI (ChatGPT Free)** — Useful for manual testing before API use
- **Tally.so** — Unlimited forms, logic branching, and simple embed
- **Make.com** — 1,000 free operations/month (ideal for MVPs)
- **Airtable** — Base tier includes automations and enough rows for prototypes
- **Notion** — Free for personal use; can function as storage, delivery, and dashboard
- **Beehiiv** — Free newsletter platform with monetization features
- **Canva** — Free tier supports branded visuals, templates, and marketing assets

Best Practice Insight: Build the first $500 in revenue using free tools. Use the profits to upgrade—*not the other way around.*

Real-World Example: From Bloat to Profit in 21 Days

What Happened

Claire launched an AI-powered resume builder. She started with:

- ChatGPT for text generation
- Typeform for inputs
- Zapier for automation
- PDFMonkey for resume output
- Stripe + Gumroad for payments
- Notion for delivery
- Mailchimp for email

She was paying over $200/month—and the system broke every two weeks.

She rebuilt using:

- Tally for form and conditional logic
- Make for AI calls, formatting, and delivery
- ChatGPT API for generation
- Notion for storage and file delivery
- Outseta for payments and email

New monthly cost: $34
Support issues: Near-zero
Conversion rate: Up 40% due to improved UX
Monthly revenue: ~$1,900 (after expenses)

What We Learn From It
Less is more. Claire didn't need *more tools*. She needed *fewer tools with better integration*. Her simplified system was faster, more stable, and more profitable.

Tactical Best Practices

- **Map before you subscribe**: Plan your tech stack on paper first. Don't buy until you know what goes where.
- **Choose tools that integrate**: Native integrations reduce the need for extra middleware (Zapier, Pabbly, etc.)
- **Stay API-aware**: Even if you're non-technical, ensure your tools support future API or webhook connections.
- **Avoid "just in case" tools**: If you're not using it today, don't pay for it yet.
- **Track ROI monthly**: Know what you're spending, what revenue each tool supports, and whether it's worth it.

Checklist-Style Action Steps

- List every paid tool you're currently using (and its function)
- Identify overlaps—can any be replaced or eliminated?
- Map your workflow (input → process → output → delivery) and assign one tool per function
- Confirm each tool has the integration/API support you'll need later
- Set a max monthly stack budget based on current revenue stage (e.g., 10% of MRR)
- Use free tiers and "stack-light" until your system earns
- Re-evaluate your stack quarterly—cut what's unused or replaceable

The Lean Stack Philosophy

Building with AI doesn't mean buying every shiny tool. It means **orchestrating the minimum number of tools to produce the maximum amount of value**.

You don't need a subscription to 15 platforms. You need one tool that solves a real problem for a real user—and a system that delivers it cleanly, reliably, and affordably.

The winners in this space aren't the ones with the biggest toolkits. They're the ones who build smart, run lean, and scale systems—not complexity.

CHAPTER 3

AI-Driven Content Publishing

Niche Site & Blog Creation With SEO Optimization

In the age of AI, content is still king—but distribution is the kingdom. Building a niche site or blog remains one of the most powerful, compounding ways to generate semi-passive income. When done right, a well-positioned blog can drive targeted traffic, capture leads, build trust, and convert readers into buyers—*without paid ads or daily maintenance.*

But here's the catch: most AI-driven blogs fail. Why? Because they chase volume instead of *value.* They publish generic content, ignore search intent, and burn out trying to compete with massive content farms.

The new opportunity lies in using AI not to flood the internet with noise, but to create **high-quality, search-optimized content in underserved niches**—strategically, sustainably, and profitably.

In this section, you'll learn how to build a niche content engine that ranks, converts, and earns—using a lean AI + SEO workflow that any non-technical founder can deploy.

Why Niche Sites Still Work Today

Despite AI saturation, Google and other search engines still prioritize content that:

- Answers specific search queries clearly
- Demonstrates topical authority over time
- Loads fast and provides a good user experience
- Attracts natural engagement, backlinks, and time-on-site

The key is **focus**. Generalist blogs get buried. Niche blogs win.

Instead of trying to rank for "best AI tools," you might target:

- "AI tools for Etsy shop owners"
- "How to write a legal clause using AI"
- "Prompt engineering for HR teams"
- "AI for church admin workflows"

This is where AI gives you leverage—not by mass-producing junk, but by helping you **go deep into micro-markets with consistent quality.**

The Passive Income Potential of Niche Blogs

When built correctly, a niche blog can earn through:

- **Affiliate marketing**: Link to tools, software, or courses with referral commissions
- **Info product sales**: Link to your own digital templates, ebooks, or courses
- **Newsletter monetization**: Capture emails and promote sponsors or premium content
- **Service upsells**: Funnel readers into a paid offer (e.g., audits, consulting, templates)
- **Ad revenue**: With enough traffic, monetize through networks like Ezoic or Mediavine

Unlike social media, SEO traffic is *evergreen*. A well-ranked post can bring consistent traffic and income for *years*—especially in underserved keyword spaces.

Step-by-Step: Building a Niche Site With AI + SEO

Step 1: Identify a Monetizable Niche

Look for:

- A *specific* audience with unmet needs (e.g., AI for lawyers, email marketing for therapists)
- Products or tools you can recommend (affiliate or own)
- Questions people are actively searching for (use Google Autosuggest, Reddit, AnswerThePublic)

Avoid niches that are:

- Oversaturated (tech news, general AI tools, finance advice)
- Lacking commercial intent (traffic with no buyers)

Pro Tip: Cross two interests. "AI for [industry]" or "No-code for [role]" often yields highly monetizable angles.

Step 2: Build the Site Fast With Lean Tools

Use platforms that prioritize **speed, SEO, and simplicity**:

- **Typedream** or **Softr** for fast, SEO-optimized websites with zero code
- **Framer** if you want more design control
- **WordPress** (with Kadence or GeneratePress) if going traditional

Ensure:

- Clean URLs and meta tags
- Mobile responsiveness
- Fast load times
- Clear CTA on every page (email opt-in, product, etc.)

Step 3: Plan SEO-Driven Content Strategy

Use tools like:

- **LowFruits.io** – Find long-tail keywords with low competition
- **AlsoAsked.com** – Discover how people ask questions in your niche
- **Keywords Everywhere** – See search volume right in Google
- **SurferSEO** or **Frase** – Optimize AI-written posts for on-page SEO

Organize content by intent:

- **Informational** (how-to, tutorials, comparisons)
- **Transactional** (reviews, "best of" lists, product roundups)
- **Navigational** (brand terms, tool walkthroughs)

Target **clusters** of content—groups of posts around one topic—to build topical authority.

Step 4: Generate High-Quality Content With AI + Editorial Oversight

Use **ChatGPT (GPT-4)** or **Claude** to draft articles, but add:

- Manual intros with real examples or case studies
- SEO-optimized headings, slugs, and meta descriptions
- Internal links to related content
- Custom call-to-actions (download, subscribe, buy)

Avoid:

- Publishing raw AI output without edits
- Ignoring readability and structure
- Stuffing keywords unnaturally

Best Practice: Use AI for first drafts, outlines, FAQs, and comparisons. You add the polish, examples, and formatting.

Step 5: Launch With 5–10 Pillar Articles

Start with:

- 3–5 **pillar posts** (1,500–2,500 words) targeting main keywords
- 5–10 **supporting articles** (500–1,200 words) targeting related long-tail searches
- 1 clear **lead magnet** (checklist, email course, AI prompt bundle) to capture emails

Link between articles. Include visuals if possible. Use Notion, Canva, or Midjourney to generate simple branded graphics.

Real-World Example: AI-Powered Niche Blog to $3,400/Month in 6 Months

What Happened

Matt, a freelance marketer, launched a niche blog: **AIforWeddingPros.com**. He targeted wedding photographers, planners, and florists looking to save time with AI.

He published:

- 12 articles in the first 30 days (all drafted with ChatGPT and optimized manually)
- A lead magnet ("7 ChatGPT Prompts for Wedding Emails")
- Reviews of AI scheduling and design tools
- Weekly AI use-case newsletter (free via Beehiiv)

He monetized through:

- Affiliate links to Calendly, Jasper, Canva Pro
- A $49 prompt bundle for client communication
- A $99 workshop replay on "AI Workflows for Creatives"

By month 6:

- Organic traffic: 9,000/month
- Email list: 2,200
- Monthly income: $3,400 (70% digital products, 30% affiliate)

What We Learn From It

Matt didn't chase traffic. He chased **intent**. By going narrow, solving specific problems, and building trust, he created an AI blog that delivers real income—not vanity metrics.

Common Mistakes That Kill Niche Blog ROI

- **Choosing topics without monetization intent**
- **Publishing AI content with no editing or strategy**
- **Chasing high-volume keywords with heavy competition**
- **Forgetting to capture emails**
- **Not linking between posts (no SEO structure)**
- **Trying to be everything to everyone**

Tactical Best Practices

- **Start small, go deep**: Choose one clear audience and build 10–15 posts before branching out
- **Use internal linking from day one**: It helps SEO and keeps users engaged
- **Repurpose content**: Turn articles into emails, YouTube scripts, PDFs
- **Test monetization early**: Don't wait for 10k visitors—add a product or offer now

- **Track rankings and refine**: Use Google Search Console and Ahrefs/WebCEO to spot opportunities

Checklist-Style Action Steps

- Define a profitable niche with commercial search intent
- Validate 10–15 low-competition, high-intent keywords
- Choose a lean website builder (Typedream, Softr, or WordPress)
- Plan 3 pillar posts and 5+ supporting articles
- Use AI to draft content, then manually optimize for SEO and tone
- Create a lead magnet and email opt-in
- Set up Google Search Console and track early performance
- Publish, promote, refine, and repeat

The Long Game: SEO Compounds, So Build Smart

The beauty of a niche blog is compounding leverage. Each article is a mini-asset—working 24/7 to rank, educate, and convert. Over time, a smartly-structured site becomes a magnet for traffic and trust.

The goal isn't to publish 500 posts. It's to publish 50 **high-value**, optimized, monetizable posts that keep working for you—*without ongoing effort.*

Newsletter Publishing and Substack Monetization

Email is still the most profitable channel in digital marketing, and newsletters—especially niche, value-driven ones—are undergoing a major renaissance. With AI at your side, launching and monetizing a newsletter is no longer reserved for experienced writers or media companies. You don't need a big list. You don't need to be an influencer. You just need to *deliver something specific and valuable to a specific group of people—consistently.*

Platforms like **Substack, Beehiiv**, and **ConvertKit** now make it possible for solo founders to turn a weekly email into a revenue-generating asset in under 30 days. But as with anything in the AI gold rush, strategy matters more than speed.

This section covers how to build, grow, and monetize a newsletter using AI-enhanced workflows—without drowning in content creation, tech overwhelm, or audience burnout.

Why Newsletters Are Still the Ultimate Digital Asset

A newsletter gives you:

- **Direct access to your audience** (no algorithms, no pay-to-play)
- **Full ownership** of the relationship and the platform
- **Recurring revenue potential** via paid subscriptions, sponsors, or product sales
- **Built-in distribution** with viral sharing, referral loops, and archivable content

Unlike blogs or social media, email builds *compounding attention.* Every subscriber is a potential customer, referral, or advocate. Every edition you send strengthens that connection.

Best of all, AI can help you **curate, write, summarize, design, and personalize**—so you can spend less time writing, and more time building your system.

Substack vs. Alternatives: Which Should You Use?

Feature	Substack	Beehiiv	ConvertKit
Ideal For	Creators, writers	Marketers, founders	Coaches, product sellers
Free Tier	Yes (generous)	Yes	Yes
Monetization Options	Paid subs + sponsors	Subscriptions, ads	Products + email funnels
SEO/Public Archive	Yes	Yes	Limited
Referral System	Yes	Yes	No
AI Integration	Manual, via GPT	Some built-in tools	GPT add-ons via Zapier

Recommendation:
Start with **Substack** if your goal is paid subscriptions or long-form content with low tech overhead.
Use **Beehiiv** if you want better analytics, referral growth, or ad network monetization.
Use **ConvertKit** if you're selling products, coaching, or building advanced email automations.

Newsletter Monetization Models (and Which to Start With)

There are three primary ways to make money from your newsletter:

1. **Paid Subscriptions**
   - Charge for premium issues, member-only content, tools, or behind-the-scenes access
   - Best for niches with clear pain points or insider value
   - Example: "$10/month for advanced AI prompts for accountants"

2. **Affiliate Monetization**
   o Promote software, tools, or courses with your referral link
   o Best for newsletters with a tools/resources angle
   o Example: "5 Best CRM Tools for Solopreneurs (and how I use them)"
3. **Sponsorships & Ads**
   o Brands pay to be featured in your newsletter
   o Requires higher volume (1k+ active readers minimum)
   o Use marketplaces like Paved or ConvertKit Sponsorship Network

Best Practice:
Start with **affiliate or product offers**, then layer in paid tiers or sponsorships once your list grows.

How to Use AI to Streamline Newsletter Creation

AI doesn't replace your voice—it *amplifies your workflow*. Use it to:

- **Curate content**: Feed URLs or topics to ChatGPT to summarize industry news
- **Generate subject lines**: Use GPT-4 to create 10 headline variations with different tones
- **Draft sections**: Give your rough notes or bullet points and let AI structure your ideas
- **Repurpose content**: Turn blog posts into newsletter editions, or newsletters into Twitter threads
- **Personalize emails**: Use variables and conditional blocks to adapt content to each reader's behavior or preference

Tools:

- **ChatGPT (GPT-4)** — for drafting, outlining, summarizing
- **Claude** — for long-context editorial planning
- **Lex.page** — a writing platform with AI assistance

- **Zapier** — to automate sending, tagging, or segmenting based on reader behavior

Real-World Example: $4,200/Month From a One-Person Newsletter

What Happened

Dani, a content strategist, launched a Substack called *PromptCraft*, focused on AI workflows for solo entrepreneurs. Her format:

- Free weekly email with 3 prompt examples and short use-case breakdowns
- Monthly premium post ($8/month or $80/year) with advanced templates, SOPs, and walkthroughs
- Automated welcome series built in ConvertKit to nurture new readers

She grew to 3,000 free subs in 90 days using:

- LinkedIn repurposed content
- Reddit posts in niche automation forums
- Cross-promotions with other Substack creators
- A GPT-powered landing page that showed a sample prompt based on visitor input

By month four:

- 330 paid subscribers
- Monthly income: ~$2,600 from subs, $1,600 from affiliate referrals
- Time invested: ~6–8 hours/week, including editing and AI prompting

What We Learn From It

Dani didn't chase scale—she chased value. She focused on a *clear promise* ("Get better prompts that make you money"), a *repeatable format*, and a *lean system*. AI didn't create her content. It enabled consistency and speed.

Common Mistakes in Newsletter Monetization

- **Starting with monetization before building trust**
- **Publishing inconsistent formats (no rhythm or voice)**
- **Chasing viral topics instead of serving a real audience**
- **Letting AI write too much without editing**
- **Focusing only on content, not list growth or engagement**

Tactical Best Practices

- **Choose a format and stick to it**: Example — "3 tools, 1 use case, 1 prompt every Tuesday"
- **Collect emails early, often, and everywhere**: Blog, social, YouTube, tools—every asset should point to your list
- **Use segmentation**: Tag people who click, buy, or refer. Send targeted upgrades or offers
- **Promote your archive**: Use public posts to boost SEO and drive discovery
- **Include clear CTAs in every issue**: Don't assume people know what to do next

Checklist-Style Action Steps

- Choose a newsletter platform (Substack, Beehiiv, or ConvertKit)
- Define your niche and value proposition in one sentence
- Plan your first 4–6 newsletter editions (theme, format, call-to-action)
- Use ChatGPT to help draft and structure your first issues
- Set up a landing page with a compelling opt-in
- Create a free lead magnet or incentive (e.g., "Free Prompt Pack")
- Publish your first edition and promote it across 2–3 organic channels

- Monitor open rates, click-throughs, and subscriber feedback weekly
- Launch your paid tier or affiliate links after your first 500–1,000 subs

The Newsletter Flywheel

Newsletters are slow at first—but powerful over time. With consistent publishing and smart automation, you build:

- Trust → Engagement
- Engagement → Conversions
- Conversions → Revenue
- Revenue → More resources to grow

Each edition is an asset. Each subscriber is a potential customer. And each workflow you automate reduces the friction of scale.

AI-Powered Authority Books & Kindle Strategies

Publishing a book has always been one of the fastest ways to build authority, grow an audience, and unlock income streams through digital products, speaking, coaching, or consulting. But traditionally, the process was slow, expensive, and filled with gatekeepers.

Today, AI has completely democratized this space. With the right tools and strategy, you can write, publish, and monetize a **high-impact authority book** in 30–60 days—even if you're not a writer. Even better, once published, your book becomes an *evergreen lead magnet, trust builder, and passive income source*—working for you 24/7 across platforms like Amazon Kindle, Audible, and Gumroad.

But like everything in the AI era, success doesn't come from automation alone. It comes from **positioning, structure, and real value**.

This section walks you through how to plan, write, and monetize a nonfiction AI-powered book that builds your brand *and* your bank account.

Why Authority Books Still Work in a Noisy Digital World

In 2025, attention is fragmented. But books still cut through— because they signal **expertise, commitment, and depth**.

A book:

- Boosts your perceived credibility instantly
- Opens doors to press, speaking, podcasts, and partnerships
- Attracts better clients (books filter by relevance and readiness)
- Builds trust at scale—readers spend hours with your voice
- Creates a lead funnel you don't have to constantly manage

Unlike tweets or blog posts, books are *anchoring assets*. You create them once—and they build trust, influence, and income for years.

Step-by-Step: How to Create a High-Trust Book With AI

Step 1: Choose a Profitable, Positioning-Aligned Topic

Don't write about AI in general. Choose a **tight problem** for a **specific audience**:

- "AI for Freelance Designers"
- "Prompt Engineering for HR Managers"
- "Using AI to Automate Agency Onboarding"
- "Passive Income With No-Code and AI Tools"

Ask yourself:

- Does this book solve a painful, money-related problem?
- Does it attract the kind of clients, customers, or audience I want?
- Will readers finish and say, "That was useful—I want more"?

AI helps you *write*, but only *strategy* makes it sell.

Step 2: Plan the Book With a Repeatable Framework

Use AI to outline, but you guide the structure. A simple and effective nonfiction format:

1. **The Problem** — What's broken in the reader's world
2. **The Shift** — New tools, mindset, or opportunity (AI, automation, etc.)
3. **The Strategy** — Step-by-step frameworks or models
4. **The Execution** — How to apply it right now
5. **The Proof** — Case studies, data, client stories
6. **The Future** — What's next and how to stay ahead

Use ChatGPT to help expand, refine, and iterate your outline.

Prompt Tip:
"Act as a nonfiction book coach. Help me outline a book for [audience] who want to [solve X problem] using [tool or strategy]."

Step 3: Use AI to Draft—You Polish and Position

Use tools like ChatGPT or Claude to generate:

- Chapter drafts based on detailed prompts
- Lists, case studies, and how-to explanations
- FAQ sections and summaries
- Title and subtitle options
- Hooks and intro paragraphs

But never publish AI output raw. Your job is to:

- Infuse real examples, voice, and analogies
- Clean up tone, flow, and structure
- Remove repetition or fluff
- Add your own insight and judgment

AI writes fast. You write *better*.

Step 4: Design, Format, and Publish Professionally

Use these tools to turn your manuscript into a Kindle-ready asset:

- **Atticus.io** — Write and format books for Kindle + print in one place
- **Canva** — Create your book cover (follow Amazon KDP specs)
- **Reedsy** — Hire vetted editors, formatters, or designers (optional)
- **Kindle Create** — Free Amazon tool to format and preview your book

Pro tip: Publish in **three formats** for max reach:

- **Kindle eBook** — Amazon's global reach + easy discovery
- **Paperback via KDP** — Print-on-demand, no inventory needed
- **PDF download via Gumroad or your own site** — Bundle with bonuses (checklists, videos, templates)

Monetization Paths for Authority Books

Publishing the book is just the beginning. Here's how to turn it into a multi-stream revenue engine:

Monetization Path	Description	Tool Example
Amazon Sales	Direct sales from Kindle & paperback	Amazon KDP
Lead Generation	Include bonus download, checklist, or free course	Notion, ConvertKit, Outseta
Affiliate Links Inside	Promote tools/services mentioned in the book	Impact, PartnerStack
Back-End Offers	Upsell consulting, workshops, templates	Gumroad, TidyCal, Notion
Audiobook Edition	Narrate with ElevenLabs and publish via ACX or Payhip	ElevenLabs, Audacity

Every book becomes a **business funnel** when it's tied to a clear product or service ecosystem.

Real-World Example: From Book to 5-Figure Product Funnel

What Happened

Julia, an agency owner, wrote a book called *AI for Account Managers* using ChatGPT for 60% of the first draft. She spent 45 days writing and editing, hired a designer on Fiverr for the cover, and published on Amazon and Gumroad.

Inside the book, she offered:

- A free "AI SOP Toolkit" in exchange for an email
- Links to her Notion templates and Airtable dashboards
- A $197 mini-course on prompt workflows for teams

Her book:

- Sold 2,400 copies in 90 days ($7,100 from eBook + print sales)
- Grew her email list by 1,600+
- Generated $18,200 in back-end product sales
- Landed two speaking gigs and one 5-figure consulting deal

What We Learn From It

Julia didn't just write a book—she launched a *brand asset*. Her book was the top of a system, not just a piece of content.

Common Mistakes to Avoid

- **Writing without a monetization strategy**: Books should lead to offers, tools, or services
- **Using AI to replace your voice**: AI supports speed—*you* are the insight
- **Publishing without editing**: Raw AI text will sink your credibility
- **Choosing generic topics**: Niche, narrow, and painful wins
- **No clear CTA inside the book**: Every chapter should invite deeper action

Tactical Best Practices

- **Use AI to draft, not to decide**: You lead. AI assists.
- **Write for clarity, not cleverness**: Teach, don't impress.
- **Keep chapters short and actionable**: Think 800–1,500 words each.
- **End chapters with next steps or takeaways**: Give the reader momentum.
- **Repurpose content**: Turn chapters into blog posts, podcast episodes, and email content.

Checklist-Style Action Steps

- Define your niche, audience, and monetization path
- Use ChatGPT or Claude to draft a 6–10 chapter outline
- Write the first 1–2 chapters using AI + human editing
- Choose a formatting tool (Atticus, Kindle Create, Reedsy)
- Design your cover using Canva or hire via Fiverr
- Publish on Amazon KDP (Kindle + paperback)
- Create a lead magnet to collect emails from readers
- Add affiliate links, bonus content, and a call to action
- Promote via newsletter, blog, or relevant communities
- Track income and repurpose content weekly

Books That Build Business

An AI-powered book isn't just an income stream—it's a **trust signal**. It works when you're offline. It builds relationships before your first conversation. It's a funnel, a filter, and a credibility multiplier.

Write the book once. Let it open doors for years.

Repurposing Content Across Multiple Platforms

In the AI era, creating content is easy—but **creating leverage** is the real game. If you're writing blog posts, recording podcasts, or sending newsletters and only using that content *once*, you're leaving value on the table.

Content repurposing is how solo founders, creators, and digital entrepreneurs punch above their weight. It's not about doing more—it's about **squeezing every drop of value from what you already made**, then distributing it across multiple platforms where your audience is already paying attention.

With AI-powered tools, you can now turn one idea into a full content ecosystem—efficiently, consistently, and without hiring a team.

This section will show you how to build a **repurposing engine** that expands your reach, increases monetization opportunities, and fuels every income stream in your AI asset stack.

Why Repurposing Works (and Why Most Skip It)

Repurposing lets you:

- **Reach new audiences** without creating from scratch
- **Match content to platform-native formats** (e.g., YouTube vs. Twitter vs. Medium)
- **Keep your messaging consistent across channels**
- **Maximize ROI on every hour spent creating**
- **Fill your content calendar weeks in advance—with less effort**

Most creators skip repurposing because they:

- Feel like they're "repeating" themselves
- Don't have a system for reformatting
- Don't understand what type of content works best *where*
- Try to do it all manually, which leads to burnout

The fix? A **repeatable, AI-assisted workflow** that turns one high-value piece into many.

The Repurposing Flywheel: One Core, Many Outputs

Start with a **core content asset**—a blog post, newsletter issue, podcast episode, or video—and spin it into multiple platform-native formats.

Example: Starting with a long-form blog post
→ Repurpose into:

- **LinkedIn carousel**: Key insights or frameworks
- **Twitter thread**: 7–10 tweet breakdown
- **Short-form video**: 60-second summary or hook (using AI voice + visuals)
- **Email campaign**: Highlight one section with a CTA
- **Notion doc or prompt pack**: Bonus download
- **Quora or Reddit post**: Answer a related question using adapted copy
- **Slide deck**: For workshops or webinar repackaging
- **Podcast outline**: Based on the post, then link back for SEO

Best Tools for AI-Powered Repurposing

Tool	Use Case	Why It Works
ChatGPT (GPT-4)	Summaries, rephrasing, content slicing	Easily turns long-form into digestible segments
Descript	Audio/video editing, podcast to clips	Transcribe + edit visually, export social snippets
Pictory	Turn text into videos (faceless or voiced)	Create video summaries with AI voice + B-roll
Typeframes	Auto-generate short videos from tweets	Great for making visual content from text
Canva	Design carousels, infographics, covers	Templates for platform-native designs
Hypefury / TweetHunter	Schedule and recycle Twitter content	Helps extend content life and automate growth
Beehiiv / Substack	Turn content into newsletters	Native formatting + segmentation options

Prompt Tip:
"Take this 1,200-word blog post and create a LinkedIn carousel outline, a 10-tweet thread, and a 1-minute video script summarizing the key points."

Real-World Example: Turning One Newsletter Into $4,500+ in Monthly Income

What Happened

Chris publishes a weekly newsletter on *AI for copywriters*. Instead of moving on after each issue, he:

1. **Creates** a long-form newsletter using ChatGPT + personal examples
2. **Repurposes** each edition into:
   - A 5-tweet thread with links
   - A 45-second video summary using Pictory + ElevenLabs
   - A downloadable Notion doc ("Prompt Pack of the Week")
   - A blog post on Medium for SEO
   - A carousel for LinkedIn
3. **Distributes** the content across Twitter, LinkedIn, YouTube Shorts, Reddit, and Quora
4. **Monetizes** via affiliate links in the Notion doc + a $9/month paid newsletter tier

Results After 5 Months:

- 6,200 newsletter subscribers
- $3,800/month in recurring revenue
- $700–$1,200/month in affiliate commissions
- 5 hours/week of total content work (thanks to AI automation)

What We Learn From It

Chris didn't scale content creation. He scaled **distribution and format**—turning *one solid idea* into a full-funnel ecosystem.

Platform-Specific Repurposing Tips

LinkedIn

- Use frameworks and case studies from your original content
- Turn steps or lessons into carousel slides (use Canva or PowerPoint)
- CTA: "Want the full guide? It's in my newsletter."

Twitter/X

- Focus on punchy insights and threads
- Use AI to rewrite paragraphs as one-liners or hooks
- CTA: "This is from my post on X—DM me 'guide' for the full PDF."

YouTube Shorts / TikTok

- Use AI to script 30–60 second summaries with a hook + 1 actionable tip
- Add visuals via Canva or use Pictory to auto-generate video
- CTA: Link to full version in the description

Email

- Highlight the most clicked or replied-to section from another platform
- Use reader replies to generate future content
- Create "highlight editions" that recap your best 3–5 repurposed posts

Reddit & Quora

- Rewrite long-form posts into direct answers for niche communities
- Add depth or examples to stand out from AI spam
- Include links to gated downloads or relevant lead magnets

Common Mistakes That Kill Repurposing ROI

- **Trying to repurpose everything manually**
- **Posting the same format everywhere (copy/paste)**
- **Ignoring platform tone and norms**
- **Skipping the CTA or lead magnet**
- **Not tracking which formats actually perform**

Tactical Best Practices

- **Create first for depth, then edit for breadth**
- **Choose 2–3 core platforms** (not 10) and repurpose strategically
- **Build templates for recurring post types** (e.g., "5 prompts," "1-minute how-to")
- **Batch your repurposing weekly**—schedule it, don't wing it
- **Track platform ROI**—which formats bring leads, revenue, or reach?

Checklist-Style Action Steps

- Choose your *core* content format (newsletter, blog, video, etc.)
- Plan 3–5 repurposing formats for each post
- Build templates for each platform (carousels, threads, scripts)
- Use AI to help format and rewrite based on platform tone
- Schedule posts using Buffer, Hypefury, or native platform tools
- Track top-performing repurposed posts by engagement + conversions

- Refine your system monthly—cut what's not working, double down on what is

Repurposing Is How You Outlast, Not Outwork

You don't need to publish more. You need to **publish smarter**. Every piece of content you create should have multiple lives. With AI and simple templates, one great idea can become **a blog post, a lead magnet, a video, a tweetstorm, and a product teaser**—all in under an hour.

Content without distribution is wasted effort. Repurposing is how you give your ideas the reach—and the revenue—they deserve.

CHAPTER 4

AI in Stock Media & Licensing

Selling AI Images on Stock Platforms

The demand for high-quality visual content has never been higher—and with AI image generation tools now accessible to solo creators, a new window of opportunity has opened: **selling AI-generated images on stock platforms**.

You no longer need to be a professional photographer or graphic designer. With the right prompts, tools, and positioning, you can create and license AI images that meet the needs of marketers, bloggers, e-commerce sellers, app developers, educators, and content creators worldwide.

This is not about art for art's sake. It's about **creating commercially valuable image assets** that solve specific content needs—and monetizing them across multiple stock marketplaces.

Done right, this can become a compounding, semi-passive income stream that scales without inventory, logistics, or client work.

Why Stock Image Sales Still Work

Despite the flood of free visuals and user-generated content, stock marketplaces remain **one of the most reliable ways to license visual content at scale**.

Why?

- Businesses need royalty-free images for marketing, products, and UI
- Content creators want legally safe, brand-aligned assets
- Marketers and agencies need fast access to diverse visuals
- Niche stock imagery (underrepresented industries, roles, or demographics) is in high demand

If your images solve a *specific visual need,* they can sell for years across platforms like Shutterstock, Adobe Stock, Creative Market, and niche directories.

AI allows you to create **volume with variation**—a huge advantage in a world where content is produced faster than ever.

What Kind of AI Images Sell?

Not all AI images are created equal. The most profitable stock content is:

- **Utility-driven**: It solves a specific need—e.g., a blog header, product mockup, medical scene
- **Commercial-safe**: It avoids logos, celebrities, and realistic likenesses of real people
- **Keyword-optimized**: It's easy to find in platform searches
- **Context-ready**: It fits into presentations, ads, social media, or websites
- **Niche-targeted**: It serves underrepresented audiences, professions, or use cases

High-Performing Categories:

- Business settings (e.g., meetings, strategy, remote work, diversity in tech)
- Medical and health scenes (e.g., doctor-patient interactions, mental health)
- Education and e-learning (e.g., students, remote classrooms, online testing)
- Abstract tech visuals (e.g., data, cybersecurity, neural networks)
- UI/UX and device mockups (e.g., app on phone, dashboard on laptop)
- Print-on-demand friendly artwork (e.g., minimalist illustrations, abstract landscapes)

Business   Medical   Tech

Education   Abstract

Top Platforms That Accept AI-Generated Content

Not all stock platforms accept AI images yet—and some have strict guidelines. Here are the major ones to know:

Platform	AI Image Policy	Revenue Model	Payout Threshold
Adobe Stock	Accepts AI images with clear labeling	Per download + bonus	$25
Shutterstock	Accepts AI if high-quality & model-safe	Revenue share per use	$35
Creative Market	Accepts digital products, bundles	You set pricing	$20
Wirestock	Distributes to multiple stock sites	Revenue share	$30
Dreamstime	Accepts AI if it meets editorial criteria	Per image license	$100
Etsy	Not a stock site, but great for POD art	Direct sales	Immediate

Pro Tip: Start with **Wirestock** to test quality—it distributes your content to multiple marketplaces with one upload and handles tagging and keywording.

AI Tools for Image Generation and Optimization

Purpose	Tool	Why Use It
Image Creation	Midjourney, DALL·E, Leonardo.ai	High-quality, prompt-driven generation
Image Upscaling	Topaz Gigapixel, Let's Enhance	Make images print or platform-ready
Background Removal	Remove.bg, Canva Pro	Clean visuals for ecommerce use
EXIF Metadata Editor	XnView, Lightroom	Embed image data, title, keywords
Prompt Testing	Krea.ai, PromptHero	Explore trending prompt styles

Best Practice: Generate at 1024×1024 or higher resolution when possible. Stock platforms often require minimum image dimensions and DPI (typically 300+ for print).

Real-World Example: $1,200/Month With AI-Generated Stock Packs

What Happened

Luis, a remote UX designer, began using Midjourney to generate mockups for client proposals. He noticed a demand for abstract tech illustrations and business concept art.

He created a series of:

- "Diverse Remote Teams" packs
- "AI Brainstorming Scenes"
- "Startup Culture Flat Lay Backgrounds"
- "Cybersecurity Concept Art"

He upscaled his images, added metadata, and uploaded via Wirestock to Adobe Stock, Shutterstock, and Dreamstime.

In the first 6 months:

- 270+ images sold across platforms
- ~$1,200/month in recurring income
- His top 20 images made up 60% of sales
- He later bundled niche collections and sold them on Gumroad and Creative Market for additional revenue

What We Learn From It

Luis succeeded because he:

- Focused on **business-friendly, utility-driven visuals**
- Used **prompt variations** to create full packs (not one-off images)
- Uploaded **consistently** with keyword optimization
- Monetized the same images **across multiple channels**

Common Mistakes to Avoid

- **Using AI images that look surreal, broken, or uncanny**
- **Violating platform guidelines (e.g., using real likenesses or logos)**
- **Failing to add metadata or relevant keywords**
- **Uploading generic content (e.g., "AI robot head") with no context**
- **Only posting one image at a time instead of collections**

Tactical Best Practices

- **Create themed image packs** (5–10 images per topic) for cohesive uploads
- **Use specific prompts**: "Minimalist tech dashboard on laptop, 3D render, isometric, clean background"
- **Upscale and sharpen every image** before submission
- **Use strong titles and searchable tags** (e.g., "Remote work diversity team meeting Zoom illustration")
- **Test in Wirestock first** before uploading directly to Adobe/Shutterstock
- **Track your top-selling styles** and iterate with variations or updated themes

Checklist-Style Action Steps

- Choose 3–5 commercial niches (business, education, tech, etc.)
- Generate 10–20 high-resolution AI images per theme
- Upscale and format images to meet platform specs
- Add titles, tags, and descriptions using keyword research
- Upload to Wirestock or direct stock platforms
- Track sales and optimize based on demand trends
- Repurpose bestsellers into bundles on Etsy or Gumroad
- Repeat with seasonal, topical, or industry-specific variations

Think Like a Stock Creator, Not an Artist

Stock platforms reward consistency, relevance, and commercial value—not artistic experimentation. Your goal isn't to impress—it's to **solve a visual problem at scale**. AI gives you the tools. The marketplace gives you the audience. Your job is to build image assets that **work in real-world use cases**.

This is where creativity meets commerce—and where AI gives you leverage without labor.

AI Music & Soundscapes for Licensing Libraries

The rise of AI in the creative space isn't limited to text and visuals—it's now transforming **music and audio production** as well. With the right tools, non-musicians and solo entrepreneurs can now create **original, royalty-free music and ambient soundscapes** that meet real commercial demand.

Think: background music for podcasts, meditation apps, YouTube videos, ads, games, and indie films. These buyers don't want chart-topping hits—they want clean, well-structured, mood-specific audio that they can **license legally, quickly, and affordably**.

AI lets you produce that content at scale—without instruments, recording gear, or audio engineering skills.

In this section, we'll show you how to create, refine, and monetize AI-generated music and soundscapes across **royalty-free licensing platforms**, while avoiding the common pitfalls that tank most uploads.

Why AI Music Is a Real Income Opportunity

Most stock audio buyers aren't looking for the next Beethoven. They're looking for:

- A relaxing 30-minute ambient loop for their meditation app
- A 10-second intro for their video podcast
- Background music that doesn't distract from narration
- Atmospheric tension beds for game development
- Branded sound logos or UI notification sounds

What matters most is:

- **Mood fit** (Does it match the vibe?)
- **Usability** (Is it clean, loopable, non-intrusive?)
- **Licensing clarity** (No hidden rights issues)
- **Metadata** (Tagged properly for search and filtering)

This is where AI excels: producing genre-specific, ready-to-license tracks at scale.

Who Buys AI-Generated Music?

- **Content creators** (YouTube, TikTok, podcasts, streamers)
- **App developers** (meditation, productivity, games, fitness)
- **Corporate video teams** (internal presentations, ads)
- **Indie filmmakers** (shorts, trailers, doc projects)
- **SaaS startups** (onboarding videos, explainer walkthroughs)

They need music—but they **don't want to pay $1,000+ for a custom track**. If you can offer clean, usable audio that solves a specific need, they'll buy it.

Top Platforms That Accept AI-Generated Audio

Platform	Accepts AI Music?	Model	Notes
Pond5	Yes (with rights clarity)	Per-download sales	Huge marketplace, strong in corporate & film
AudioJungle	Yes (high quality only)	Pay-per-license	Emphasis on usability, metadata-rich uploads
SoundCloud Pro	Yes (for direct licensing)	Direct sales + fan support	Ideal for building a brand around your audio

Platform	Accepts AI Music?	Model	Notes
Bandcamp	Yes (manual licensing)	Direct-to-audience	Good for selling packs, albums, or bundles
Epidemic Sound	No direct AI submissions	Curated contributors only	Closed ecosystem—apply if you reach scale
BeatStars	Yes (esp. for loops & beats)	Beat licensing	Great for shorter loops, intros, or music beds

Pro Tip: Use **Pond5** or **AudioJungle** to test demand—then cross-sell via **Bandcamp** or direct on **Gumroad** for bundled offers.

Best AI Tools for Audio & Music Creation

Tool	Use Case	Why Use It
Soundraw	Auto-generate royalty-free tracks	Easy for non-musicians, customize moods/styles
AIVA	Compose cinematic, ambient, classical	Strong for film, podcast, and game scores
Boomy	Instant track generation + distribution	Great for testing music styles and publishing
Mubert Render	Looping AI music for commercial use	Ideal for meditation, productivity, tech vibes
Endlesss / Amper (legacy)	Collaborative AI sound design	For beat makers and experimental producers
Adobe Audition / Audacity	Post-processing & mastering	Clean up, fade, normalize audio before upload

Prompt Tip:
"Create a 2-minute ambient loop in minor key, minimal instrumentation, good for background in a mobile productivity app."

Then refine in a DAW (digital audio workstation) for volume leveling and exporting in proper formats.

Real-World Example: Generating $900/Month With AI Sound Packs

What Happened

Eli, a UX designer, started building productivity apps and needed clean ambient tracks. He used **Mubert** and **AIVA** to generate:

- Focus music loops
- Meditation background pads
- Short notification sounds
- Branded audio stingers

He cleaned them up in **Audacity**, bundled them into:

- "30 AI-Generated Productivity Loops"
- "Calm UI Sounds for Mobile Devs"
- "Background Beds for Podcasters"

Then uploaded to **Pond5**, **Bandcamp**, and sold via **Gumroad** with commercial licenses.

After 90 days:

- Monthly income: ~$900 from licensing + direct bundle sales
- Customer base: indie devs, podcast producers, SaaS teams
- Time investment: ~5 hours/week (batch creation + uploads)
- Support: zero (products are pre-licensed and automated)

What We Learn From It

Eli didn't just "make beats"—he created **audio tools** for real business needs. By combining AI, simple editing, and smart packaging, he built a low-touch income stream with zero code or music background.

Common Mistakes in AI Music Licensing

- **Using copyrighted samples or unclear licensing tools**
- **Uploading low-quality or unedited loops**
- **Ignoring platform-specific format requirements (e.g., WAV vs. MP3)**
- **No metadata (title, mood, keywords, instruments)**
- **Creating tracks that are too short or too complex for commercial use**

Tactical Best Practices

- **Focus on mood and function**: Meditation, ambient, background, tech, cinematic
- **Use loop-friendly structures**: 1–3 minutes with seamless fades
- **Normalize volume**: Ensure consistent loudness across tracks
- **Include alternate versions**: With/without drums, short versions, stems
- **Tag with mood, genre, and usage context**: e.g., "calm, focus, productivity, background, tech"
- **Bundle by use-case**: "5 onboarding loops," "10 meditation pads," "UI sound FX pack"

Checklist-Style Action Steps

- Choose a music generation tool (e.g., Soundraw, AIVA, Mubert)
- Create 5–10 audio tracks based on niche use cases (apps, videos, meditation)

- Edit, clean, and normalize audio in Audacity or Adobe Audition
- Export in WAV and MP3 formats with proper naming conventions
- Add clear metadata: mood, instruments, genre, tempo, tags
- Upload to Pond5, AudioJungle, Bandcamp, or Gumroad
- Create themed bundles and license them as commercial-use packs
- Track performance, optimize based on what sells, and repeat

Audio as an Asset Class

AI-generated music isn't just content—it's a **digital asset**. One 2-minute loop, if well positioned, can be licensed hundreds of times across platforms. Multiply that by a dozen themes or use cases, and you have a **compounding, low-maintenance income stream**.

You don't need fame. You need functionality. Build clean, useful sound assets that solve problems for creators and businesses—and let AI accelerate the volume and variation.

Templates & Digital Design Packs for Marketplaces

If you want to build a compounding income stream without trading hours for dollars, **selling templates and digital design packs** is one of the most practical, scalable strategies in the AI creator economy. Whether you're a designer, marketer, strategist, or total beginner, today's AI tools allow you to create **ready-to-use digital assets** that businesses, freelancers, and creators are eager to buy.

From Canva templates and Notion dashboards to brand kits, slide decks, and website wireframes, these assets are in constant demand—because they **save people time**. And when your digital product saves time, improves results, or simplifies work, it becomes something people are happy to pay for.

The best part? You can build once, sell forever. When paired with smart marketplaces and the right AI workflow, a single template pack can become a long-tail asset that earns across platforms for months or years.

Why Templates Are a Top-Tier Digital Asset

Templates sell because they solve a universal problem: **"I need something done fast, and I don't want to start from scratch."**

They work especially well for:

- Solo business owners who can't afford agencies
- Freelancers who want to look pro instantly
- Coaches and consultants who need branded documents
- Ecommerce sellers looking for product mockups
- Creators launching content without design skills
- Corporate teams needing slide decks, reports, or SOPs

If you focus on *utility over creativity*, you'll win. Customers want results—not pretty fluff.

Best-Selling Types of Templates and Design Packs

Template Type	Popular Use Cases	Format Examples
Canva Templates	Social posts, brand kits, lead magnets	Instagram carousels, eBook covers
Notion Templates	Productivity, planning, client systems	Dashboards, CRMs, planners
Google Sheets/Excel	Financial models, tracking tools	Budget calculators, KPI dashboards
Slide Decks	Pitch decks, webinars, trainings	PowerPoint, Google Slides

Template Type	Popular Use Cases	Format Examples
Figma UI Kits	Startup MVPs, SaaS landing pages	Wireframes, style guides
Ebook/Lead Magnet Kits	Coaches, agencies, info-product sellers	PDF, Canva, InDesign templates
Proposal & Contract Kits	Freelancers, agencies	Doc, PDF, Notion

Pro Tip: The best-selling templates combine **great design + clear function + easy customization**.

Platforms to Sell Templates and Packs

Marketplace	Best For	Revenue Model
Creative Market	Design-driven audiences	You set pricing
Etsy	Broad audience, printables, bundles	Per product sale
Gumroad	Direct selling to your own audience	Instant delivery
Notion Marketplaces	Notion-specific (e.g. Notionery)	Commission or direct sale
Pitch	Slide decks and business templates	Niche B2B audience
UI8, Envato Elements	Figma/UI templates	Commission or licensing

Start with **Etsy or Gumroad** if you're solo. Use **Creative Market** if your design work is polished and brandable. Upload **Notion** assets to Notionery or distribute via your newsletter or social channels.

How AI Supercharges Template Creation

You don't need to design every element by hand. AI helps you:

- **Brainstorm layout structures** (ChatGPT)
- **Write placeholder or demo content** (ChatGPT, Claude)
- **Generate icons or illustrations** (DALL·E, Midjourney, Canva Magic)
- **Create color palettes or design direction** (Khroma, Coolors, GPT-4)
- **Generate instructional copy or tooltips** for Notion/SaaS/UX assets

Example Prompt:
"Give me 5 layout ideas for a Canva template pack aimed at yoga instructors promoting their classes on Instagram."

Let AI do the heavy lifting on structure and copy, so you can focus on design flow and usability.

Real-World Example: Selling $3,800/Month in Canva + Notion Packs

What Happened

Maya, a social media freelancer, started designing branded Canva templates for fitness coaches. Each pack included:

- 30 social media post templates
- A content calendar
- Brand guideline PDF
- Bonus: Lead magnet template (eBook cover + layout)

She used AI to:

- Generate captions for demo images
- Create color-coded content plans in Google Sheets

- Write tutorial copy for customers
- Test brand voice variants for niche audiences

Then she bundled the packs and listed them on **Etsy** and **Creative Market**, priced between $19–$49.

She later added:

- A **Notion-based client CRM template**
- A **pricing calculator** in Google Sheets
- A **content strategy mini-course** with purchase

Results (after 6 months):

- ~$3,800/month in average income
- 2,100 customers
- 14% return buyer rate
- <5 hours/month in support or updates

What We Learn From It

Maya didn't just sell design—she sold *speed and confidence*. Her templates gave her niche market a toolkit that *looked great and worked instantly*. AI made production faster, and bundling increased value.

Common Mistakes to Avoid

- **Overdesigning**: Complex layouts confuse. Keep it editable and simple.
- **Selling generic templates**: Niche down. "Canva template for business" = no sales.
- **Skipping instructions or guides**: Always include a PDF or Loom video walkthrough.
- **Not testing usability**: If a beginner can't edit it in under 5 minutes, it won't sell.
- **Ignoring search optimization**: Use keywords your buyer would type—e.g., "Canva pitch deck for realtors"

Tactical Best Practices

- **Focus on outcome, not format**: "Get more clients with this Notion CRM," not "Notion template"
- **Use bundle pricing**: $29 for 1, or $49 for 3 templates—encourages higher cart value
- **Add real-use demos**: Include screenshots or videos of templates in action
- **Offer both editable and final files**: Canva links + PDFs, Figma files + PNGs
- **Track what sells**: Double down on bestsellers by adding variations, updates, or upsells

Checklist-Style Action Steps

- Choose a niche (e.g., coaches, SaaS founders, Etsy sellers, agency teams)
- Define 1–2 templates that solve specific problems (e.g., client intake, content planning)
- Use AI to generate structure, placeholder copy, or design mockups
- Design in Canva, Notion, Figma, or Google Docs/Sheets
- Export in multiple formats (PDF, editable file, instructions)
- Bundle into 3–5 asset packs for higher perceived value
- Upload to Etsy, Gumroad, and Creative Market
- Optimize titles, tags, and thumbnails for search
- Promote via social, email, or bundled with your other digital products

Templates That Solve, Sell

Great design doesn't sell itself. **Templates that solve real, recurring problems do.** The sweet spot is where ease meets outcome—where your customer opens the file and immediately thinks, *"This saves me hours."*

With AI, you can build those tools faster. With smart marketplaces, you can monetize them instantly. And once published, they become **digital inventory**—earning 24/7, while you build your next asset.

Compliance With IP, Copyright, and "AI-Generated" Labels

As AI-generated content floods the internet—from text and images to music and software—so do the legal questions. What can you sell? What do you own? Do you need to disclose that your product was made using AI? And what happens if a platform flags your work?

If you're building AI-powered income streams—especially on third-party marketplaces or platforms—you must understand how **intellectual property (IP), copyright law, and platform guidelines** apply to AI-generated products.

This isn't just about staying out of legal trouble. It's about **protecting your work**, ensuring long-term monetization, and building trust with your customers.

This section gives you a practical, plain-English guide to compliance—what to watch out for, what to avoid, and how to create and sell with confidence.

Why Compliance Matters in AI-Driven Income

The explosion of generative AI has created gray areas around:

- Ownership: Who owns AI-generated content?
- Disclosure: When are you legally required to say it was AI-assisted?

- Licensing: Can you license something that AI "helped" you create?
- Risk: What happens if your work is too similar to someone else's?

When you're selling digital assets, stock media, templates, or content created or enhanced by AI, these questions aren't theoretical—they're real business risks.

Avoiding takedowns, bans, or lawsuits starts with understanding what's yours, what's not, and what needs to be clearly labeled.

1. Intellectual Property: What You *Can* and *Cannot* Own

AI models generate outputs based on patterns learned from large datasets—much of which may be copyrighted. This creates a fundamental tension:

- **You** provided the input (prompt)
- **The model** generated the output
- **The output** may or may not be legally "yours"

What You Can Typically Claim:

✅ AI-generated content you *meaningfully edited, customized, or integrated*

✅ Original compositions built on AI outputs with human creativity

✅ Works that don't infringe on anyone else's identifiable likeness, logo, or content

✅ AI-generated outputs used as *part of a larger human-made product*

What You Cannot Claim:

✖ Unedited, raw AI outputs with no creative input

✖ Content that copies style or structure of copyrighted works (e.g., "in the style of Pixar")

✘ Anything that includes **realistic portrayals of real people** (unless you have model releases)

✘ Logos, designs, or branding that look like existing trademarks

Best Practice: Treat AI as a tool, not a creator. Your legal protection comes from the *human direction and final product*, not the machine's output.

2. Copyright: Can You Register or License AI-Generated Work?

In the U.S., copyright law currently does **not recognize fully AI-generated work** as copyrightable. To be protected:

- The work must have **human authorship**
- AI can assist, but the core **creative decisions** must be yours
- You must be able to **describe your role in shaping the output**

This doesn't mean you can't sell AI-made products. It just means:

- You may not be able to stop someone from copying them unless there's clear human authorship
- Licensing is **contract-based**, not copyright-based—your terms matter

If you're selling templates, audio, art, or content:

✓ Add a license file outlining how the buyer can use the product

✓ Clearly state what is allowed (e.g., personal use, commercial use, resale limits)

✓ Keep project records (prompts, edits, versions) in case of disputes

3. "AI-Generated" Labels: When (and Where) You Must Disclose

Some platforms now **require clear labeling** of AI-generated or AI-assisted content.

Platform	Labeling Requirement	Notes
Adobe Stock	Must label as "AI-generated"	Add in title and metadata
Shutterstock	AI content allowed if original	No disclosure tag yet, but must follow guidelines
Amazon KDP	Disclosure *required* for AI content (as of 2023)	Use KDP form fields
Etsy	Encouraged, but not enforced	Transparency builds buyer trust
Substack	No formal rule (yet)	Good practice to mention if asked

Failing to disclose AI usage can lead to:

- Content takedowns
- Account suspension
- Loss of trust or refunds from customers

Rule of thumb: If the buyer would assume it's "handmade" or "human-written," and it's not—you should disclose.

4. Avoiding Risk: Logos, Faces, Styles, and Trademarks

The biggest risks in AI-generated content come from **infringement**—unintentional or not.

Avoid these high-risk areas:

⚫ **Logos and Trademarks**

- Never include brand names (e.g., Nike, Apple) in prompts
- Avoid recreating packaging, icons, or slogans
- Don't upload anything that resembles a known brand's visual identity

⚫ **Celebrity Likenesses**

- AI that "resembles" real people is risky—even if not named
- Stock platforms will reject or ban these images
- For audio/voice cloning: Never impersonate public figures

⚫ **Style Mimicry**

- Avoid prompts like "in the style of Disney, Marvel, or Picasso"
- AI outputs may get flagged as derivative work, even if subtly

Safe Prompting Alternatives:

- "Flat vector business illustration, pastel color palette"
- "Ambient electronic loop, 80 BPM, cinematic tension"
- "Professional legal document template, minimalist layout"

5. Licensing Best Practices for AI Products

If you're selling templates, visuals, or music—create your **own license terms**. This protects you *and* your buyer.

Include:

- ✓ What's allowed (commercial use, unlimited use, personal use only, etc.)
- ✓ What's prohibited (resale, redistribution, AI training, etc.)

- ✓ File types, included assets, and editing rights
- ✓ Your name or brand as the licensor

Use simple PDF or TXT files with every download, or include the license on your Gumroad, Etsy, or Creative Market listing.

Real-World Example: How a Seller Got Banned for Non-Compliance

What Happened

An Etsy seller uploaded Midjourney-generated posters labeled as "original digital art." The prints resembled a famous movie franchise's visual style but didn't directly use logos or characters.

After 200+ sales, Etsy removed the shop without warning—citing **IP infringement and deceptive listing practices**. Appeals were denied.

What Went Wrong

- The seller didn't disclose the artwork was AI-generated
- The design *evoked* a recognizable franchise (style mimicry)
- The listing described the item as "handmade digital illustration"

What We Learn From It

Even indirect resemblance or poor labeling can get your store banned. Platforms are enforcing IP policies aggressively as AI content explodes. Always err on the side of transparency and originality.

Tactical Best Practices

- **Use clear, platform-safe prompts**
- **Avoid brand names, faces, and likenesses**
- **Label AI-generated work explicitly where required**
- **Keep a changelog of your process** (prompt + edits)
- **Include licensing files for each product**
- **Monitor platform terms monthly**—they evolve quickly
- **Don't copy popular templates/styles—create your own spin**

Checklist-Style Action Steps

- Review each platform's AI content policy before uploading
- Create a simple license template for your products (reuse across all listings)
- Add "AI-generated" tags or disclaimers where required
- Avoid style prompts tied to artists, movies, or brands
- Log your prompts and editing process for every major asset
- Run a reverse image or phrase search before uploading questionable content
- Stay subscribed to updates from platforms you sell on
- Respond quickly to takedown requests or disputes with documentation

Protect the Business You're Building

Compliance isn't just about playing it safe—it's about **building a brand and product library that lasts**. AI gives you the power to create faster than ever. But if you build on shaky legal ground, everything you publish could be removed, blocked, or cloned.

Transparency builds trust. Smart prompting avoids risk. And proactive licensing ensures that what you make can keep earning—without interruption.

CHAPTER 5

AI in Self-Publishing

Kindle eBooks & Paperback Workflow

Publishing on Amazon is one of the most efficient, automated, and cost-effective ways to turn your knowledge—or AI-assisted content—into a **long-term passive income asset**. When done right, your Kindle eBook and print-on-demand paperback can generate revenue for years, while also building your authority, growing your audience, and seeding backend offers like courses, consulting, or digital products.

The key is to treat Kindle not as a place to dump low-value content, but as a **premium distribution channel**—one that rewards quality, positioning, and a clean publishing workflow. And thanks to AI, solo creators can now write, format, and publish polished books without ghostwriters, expensive editors, or complicated software.

This section gives you the **end-to-end workflow** to publish both eBook and paperback versions of your book on Amazon KDP—optimized for discoverability, credibility, and long-term monetization.

Why Kindle and Print-on-Demand Are Still Underrated

Unlike most online content channels, Amazon offers:

Global distribution (your book is available in 15+ marketplaces instantly)

Passive sales (no launch needed—books sell for years through search)

No inventory or fulfillment (paperbacks are printed on demand)

Built-in trust (Amazon reviews and rankings carry weight)

Higher perceived value (books are taken more seriously than blog posts)

A Kindle book isn't just a product—it's a **leverage engine**. It can:

Build your personal brand

Generate leads through bonus links

Unlock speaking, podcast, and media opportunities

Feed your entire AI content ecosystem

Done well, it becomes the *cornerstone asset* in your income stack.

Step-by-Step Workflow: From Manuscript to Marketplace

Step 1: Finalize Your Manuscript (Text + Structure)

Use AI to assist with:

First-draft generation (via ChatGPT, Claude, or Gemini)

Chapter outlining (keep each chapter focused and actionable)

Subheading expansion (AI can help break ideas into readable parts)

Editing passes (ask AI to shorten, clarify, or vary tone)

☑ Always include **your own insights, case studies, and real-world experience**—this is what gives your book lasting value and avoids generic fluff.

📌 **Target length**: 15,000–30,000 words for Kindle nonfiction

📌 **File format**: DOCX or Google Docs (convert later to EPUB or KPF)

Step 2: Format Your eBook for Kindle

There are two clean, low-cost formatting paths:

Atticus.io

> All-in-one tool for writing and formatting

> Creates both EPUB (for Kindle) and PDF (for print)

> Easy to add front/back matter, chapter headings, and callouts

Kindle Create (Free Amazon Tool)

> Import your DOCX

> Apply built-in themes

> Add table of contents and preview flow

> Outputs KPF file for Kindle upload

Formatting Best Practices:

> Keep fonts simple (e.g., Georgia, Garamond, or Amazon defaults)

> Add a clickable Table of Contents

> Use short paragraphs and subheadings for readability

Avoid complex graphics—use full-width images sparingly and only if necessary

End each chapter with a **next step, summary, or CTA**

Step 3: Create Your Paperback Interior

Amazon KDP lets you offer a **print-on-demand paperback** edition automatically, but the layout requirements differ slightly.

Use these tools for formatting:

Atticus.io or **Reedsy Book Editor** (auto formats for 6x9 layout)

Canva Pro (for single-column layout with bleed settings)

Vellum (Mac only—professional layout, pricey but beautiful)

Layout Tips:

Use 6" x 9" trim size (industry standard for nonfiction)

Font size: 11–12 pt

Line spacing: 1.3–1.5

Justify text (for cleaner edges)

Add page numbers, headers, and section breaks

Export as **print-ready PDF** with embedded fonts and bleed if using images.

Step 4: Design a Professional Cover

Kindle and paperback covers have different dimensions. You'll need:

eBook cover (JPG, 1600x2560 minimum)

Paperback full cover (includes front, back, spine; PDF format)

Best Tools:

Canva – Free cover templates (search "Kindle Cover")

BookBrush – Tailored for authors; includes mockups

Fiverr/Upwork – Hire affordable cover designers

Use Amazon's **KDP Cover Calculator** to get exact spine width (depends on page count).

Cover Essentials:

Strong, readable title (test at thumbnail size)

Clear subtitle that promises transformation or outcome

Consistent font and color palette

Author name (use pen name or personal brand)

Back cover: brief summary + optional photo or testimonial

Step 5: Set Up Your KDP Book Listing

Go to kdp.amazon.com and follow the guided process.

Listing Fields to Prepare:

Title & Subtitle: Use keywords, keep it promise-driven

Book Description: Format with HTML (use bold, bullets, headers)

Author Name: Use your real name or brand pen name

Keywords: 7 searchable phrases your readers would use

Categories: Choose 2 relevant BISAC categories (Amazon lets you request 8 via email post-launch)

Manuscript Upload: KPF for eBook, PDF for paperback

Cover Upload: JPG for eBook, print-ready PDF for paperback

Pricing: $2.99–$9.99 for eBook (70% royalty); $9.99–$19.99 for paperback (based on length and print costs)

Pro Tip: Use the **Look Inside** feature to showcase your table of contents and opening chapter—make it count.

Step 6: Preview and Publish

Use the **Kindle Previewer** to check how your book looks on:

Kindle Paperwhite

Kindle Fire

Phone and tablet

Print (for margins, alignment, headers, etc.)

Fix any formatting issues, then click **"Publish"**. Your book typically goes live within **24–72 hours**.

Real-World Example: Publishing a Lean Authority Book in 30 Days

What Happened

Darren, a productivity coach, used ChatGPT to help structure a book on "AI-Assisted Time Management for Remote Workers." He:

Outlined 9 chapters using AI

Wrote 1,200–1,800 words per chapter with a mix of AI + personal stories

Formatted using Atticus and designed the cover in Canva

Uploaded to Kindle as both eBook and paperback

Included a link to a bonus Notion template in the back matter

Results (first 60 days):

470 eBook downloads

78 paperback orders

180 new email subscribers via in-book lead magnet

3 clients booked coaching packages through book link

$1,860 in royalties + $5,200 in backend sales

What We Learn From It

Darren didn't just publish a book—he built an **evergreen lead engine**. The Kindle platform did the distribution, the book built trust, and the backend did the selling.

Common Mistakes to Avoid

✖ Publishing raw AI text with no human editing

✖ Using low-resolution or amateurish covers

✖ Skipping formatting—bad layouts lead to refunds and poor reviews

✖ Choosing vague, overused titles ("AI for Success")

✖ Ignoring platform-specific rules (like file formats or image DPI)

Tactical Best Practices

Start with a small, focused topic you can finish in 30–45 days

Use AI to accelerate structure, not replace thinking

Always preview before publishing—errors kill trust

Include a lead magnet or offer in your book's back matter

Promote in relevant groups, Substack, or email list post-launch

Repurpose chapters into blog posts or LinkedIn content

Checklist-Style Action Steps

Finalize book topic, target audience, and transformation

Use AI to outline and draft your manuscript (15K–30K words)

Format for Kindle using Atticus or Kindle Create

- Format paperback interior (6x9 PDF with margins and page numbers)

- Design Kindle and print covers using Canva or BookBrush

- Upload files to KDP and complete listing details

- Preview final layouts in Kindle Previewer

- Set pricing and publish

- Add bonus links to build email list or promote backend offers

- Track performance and reviews weekly, optimize listings as needed

Turn Your Book Into a System

Publishing a Kindle book isn't the end—it's the beginning of a **flywheel**. One book can fuel your content strategy, lead generation, authority positioning, and product funnel. With AI supporting the creation process and Amazon handling the fulfillment, your only job is to write with purpose—and structure your book like an asset.

Build once. Improve forever. Get paid repeatedly.

AI Audiobook Narration & Distribution

Audiobooks are the **fastest-growing format** in the publishing world, and for good reason. They offer a hands-free, screen-free way for busy professionals, commuters, and multitaskers to consume content.

For creators, they offer **another revenue stream**—often doubling or tripling the income from a single book.

Until recently, narrating an audiobook was time-consuming, expensive, and technical. But AI voice synthesis has flipped the script: you can now produce **studio-quality audiobooks** using AI narrators, at a fraction of the time and cost.

In this section, you'll learn how to use AI to convert your eBook or paperback into a compelling audiobook, publish it to major platforms, and **maximize discoverability and royalties** with minimal manual labor.

Why Audiobooks Matter for Passive Income

Audiobooks aren't just a bonus—they can outperform your Kindle or paperback editions.

Here's why:

> **Higher perceived value**: Listeners are willing to pay more
>
> **New audience segment**: Many audiobook buyers don't read eBooks
>
> **Cross-platform discoverability**: Audible, Spotify, Apple Books, and Google Play
>
> **Loyal customers**: Listeners often finish more of your content than readers
>
> **Bundling opportunities**: Sell all formats as premium packages on your website or Gumroad

If you're already creating long-form content—books, courses, newsletters—**not turning it into audio is leaving money on the table**.

Can You Use AI Voices for Commercial Audiobooks?

Yes—with caveats.

AI voice synthesis platforms have improved drastically, offering **lifelike narration with natural inflection, pacing, and emotion**. But some platforms (like Audible's ACX) still **do not accept AI-narrated books**.

So you have two options:

Use AI narration for non-Audible platforms (Google Play, Spotify, Apple Books, etc.)

Use human narration (or hybrid AI-human) if you want to publish on Audible/ACX

Good News: New platforms like **Google Play Books** and **DeepZen** allow and even support AI-narrated titles for commercial distribution.

Best AI Narration Tools for Audiobooks

Tool	Key Features	AI Voice Quality	Audible Compatible?
ElevenLabs	Ultra-realistic, emotional TTS voices	★★★★★	✖
Murf.ai	Clean narration with voice customization	★★★★☆	✖
Play.ht	Wide library of narrators, export options	★★★★☆	✖
Google Play AI Narrator	Built-in support for eBooks	★★★★☆	✅ (Google Play only)

Tool	Key Features	AI Voice Quality	Audible Compatible?
DeepZen	Human-sounding AI licensed for distribution	★★★★☆	✅ (via Findaway Voices)

Pro Tip: Use **ElevenLabs** for internal products or direct sales, and **DeepZen** or **Google Play** for wider retail publishing.

End-to-End AI Audiobook Workflow

Step 1: Finalize Your Manuscript

Remove images, links, and sidebars

Ensure your text is clean, with logical breaks and subheadings

Add a brief audio-specific introduction (optional)

Step 2: Choose a Narrator Voice

Match voice tone to your audience (e.g., calm and clear for business, energetic for lifestyle)

Use AI tools to test samples with different genders, accents, and tones

Edit the text for **spoken-word clarity** (shorter sentences, active tone)

Step 3: Generate the Narration

Use a TTS tool like ElevenLabs, Play.ht, or Murf

Break your manuscript into chapters or sections (1–3 minutes per segment)

Adjust pronunciation, pacing, and inflection using SSML tags or
in-tool settings

Step 4: Post-Process the Audio

Use **Audacity** or **Adobe Audition** to:

Normalize volume levels

Add room tone between chapters

Clean up audio artifacts

Insert music intros or outros (optional but pro-level)

Step 5: Export and Format

File format: MP3 or WAV

Bitrate: 192 kbps minimum (ACX requires specific specs)

Label files cleanly: 01_Introduction.mp3, 02_Chapter1.mp3,
etc.

Where to Publish Your AI Audiobook

Platform	AI Narration Allowed?	Royalty Rate	Notes
Google Play Books	☑ Yes (native tool)	~70%	Fastest entry point for AI audio
Kobo Writing Life	☑ Yes	45%	Global reach, no exclusivity
Spotify via Findaway	☑ (DeepZen only)	25–80%	Wide reach, use Findaway Voices
Authors Direct	☑ Yes (via Findaway)	70–80%	Direct audiobook storefront
Gumroad/Payhip	☑ Yes	90%+ (minus fees)	Sell bundles directly, include transcripts
Audible/ACX	✖ No AI narrators yet	25–40%	Requires human narration only

Real-World Example: Audiobook Launch Without Voice Talent

What Happened

Julia, a productivity consultant, wrote a short Kindle book: "Focus Systems for AI-Era Entrepreneurs." Instead of hiring a narrator, she used **Play.ht** to generate a clean, female professional voice.

She:

Broke the manuscript into 15 segments

Edited for audio flow (shorter intros, fewer lists)

Used **Audacity** to normalize levels

Added a soft ambient intro track to the beginning and end

She published the audiobook on:

Google Play Books

Gumroad (as a bonus product with her eBook)

Spotify via Findaway + DeepZen

Results in 90 days:

$2,200 in audiobook sales across platforms

480 Gumroad eBook + audio bundles

1 new consulting client per month from audiobook listeners

Less than 8 hours total production time

What We Learn From It

Julia didn't wait for studio narration. She used AI to **package her expertise as audio**, met her audience where they were (busy professionals), and gave them a convenient, high-value format.

Common Mistakes to Avoid

✖ Uploading to Audible with AI narration (auto-rejected)

✖ Using AI voices without editing for clarity

✖ Ignoring chapter breaks and pacing

✖ Poor labeling or file organization (gets flagged)

✖ Skipping preview—robotic sections kill credibility

Tactical Best Practices

Choose a consistent voice tone across the book

Edit for audio experience—eliminate jargon, long blocks, and visual cues

Add subtle intro/outro music for polish

Offer all three formats together (eBook + paperback + audio)

Bundle audio with other offers (Notion templates, checklists, course trials)

Track which chapters hold attention (use analytics from Gumroad or Spotify)

Checklist-Style Action Steps

Finalize and edit your manuscript for audio clarity

Choose an AI narration tool based on quality and distribution goals

Record or generate narration, chapter by chapter

Post-process audio: normalize, clean, segment

Format files and metadata properly for platform specs

Publish to Google Play, Kobo, Spotify (via Findaway), or Gumroad

Offer audio bundles with your Kindle or paperback editions

Promote on social, email, and inside your book's back matter

Monitor reviews, adjust tone or structure for future projects

Audio Is the Future—Make It Your Asset

The audio revolution is here, and AI puts it in your hands. With the right tools, tone, and platform strategy, you can produce audiobooks that sound professional, scale globally, and compound in value over time.

You don't need a microphone. You don't need a sound engineer. You just need a clear message, a strong structure, and a voice that your audience will trust—AI can take care of the rest.

Low-Content & Interactive Book Niches

While most people associate self-publishing with full-length novels or nonfiction books, there's a highly profitable, often overlooked opportunity in **low-content and interactive books**. These include journals, planners, activity books, logbooks, workbooks, coloring books, trackers, and educational prompts—products that deliver **value through structure and engagement**, not longform writing.

Thanks to AI tools and no-code design platforms, creators can now build entire product lines of these books—targeted, niche-specific, and printable on demand. When combined with smart keyword research and clear formatting, they become **scalable, repeatable assets** with minimal production time and long shelf lives.

In this section, we'll explore the most profitable low-content niches, how to create them using AI-enhanced workflows, and where to publish and market them for maximum results.

What Is a Low-Content or Interactive Book?

A **low-content book** is any physical or digital book where the reader contributes the content by filling in prompts, following a structure, or engaging with repeatable layouts. Your job as the creator is to design a functional, easy-to-use framework.

Examples include:

Daily planners

Meal prep logs

Mood or habit trackers

Fitness journals

Affirmation and gratitude journals

Puzzle and activity books

Learning workbooks for kids or adults

Prompt-based creativity books

Coloring books with AI-generated line art

These products are **highly giftable**, often bought in multiples, and rarely returned.

Why These Books Sell (and Resell)

The value of these books lies not in content—but in **usefulness**:

People buy them to organize, track, learn, or express

They appeal to emotion, intention, and identity ("I want to get organized," "I want to be more mindful")

They're **evergreen**—customers buy again monthly or annually

They're consumable—journals and trackers get filled, then reordered

They're great for **niche markets** with little competition but high demand

Unlike traditional books, **you don't need to be an expert**—you need to understand structure, utility, and audience language.

Profitable Niches to Explore

Niche	Example Products	Audience
Health & Wellness	Meal planners, fitness logs, water trackers	Dieters, gym-goers, wellness communities
Mental Health	Anxiety journals, gratitude logs, CBT worksheets	Therapists, self-help readers
Kids Education	Handwriting practice, math puzzles, ABC coloring	Homeschool parents, teachers
Small Business	Inventory logs, content planners, client trackers	Etsy sellers, freelancers, coaches
Spirituality	Manifestation journals, tarot spreads, moon logs	New age, astrology, meditation audiences
Creativity & Writing	Story prompts, poetry starters, sketchbooks	Writers, artists, content creators

Niche	Example Products	Audience
Hobby & Lifestyle	Garden logs, RV travel diaries, recipe books	Retirees, hobbyists, families
Special Events	Wedding planners, baby memory books, grief journals	Parents, newlyweds, support networks

Pro Tip: Choose a **hyper-specific angle**, like "Meal Prep Planner for PCOS" or "Anxiety Journal for College Students." Narrow niches lead to higher conversions.

Creating Low-Content Interiors With AI

You don't need to manually design every page. AI and design tools make it fast:

1. Prompt-Based Page Generation

Use ChatGPT to generate:

Journal prompts

Reflection questions

Daily/weekly check-ins

Educational worksheets

Structured routines or habit templates

Example Prompt:
"Generate 30 daily gratitude prompts for a mental health journal targeting women aged 30–45 dealing with anxiety."

2. Layout Design Tools

Tool	Use Case	Notes
Canva	Layout design for planners/journals	Free templates, export to PDF
BookBolt	Interior templates + KDP metadata	Built for low-content sellers
Affinity Publisher	Professional layout design	Alternative to InDesign
PowerPoint / Google Slides	Simple page layout	Great for structured pages and exports

Design one master page, then **duplicate and vary** using AI-generated prompts or categories.

3. Line Art for Activity & Coloring Books

Use tools like **Midjourney**, **DALL·E**, or **Kittl** to generate clean black-and-white illustrations.

Prompt Example:
"Line art of jungle animals for kids' coloring book, no shading, clean outlines only"

Export at 300 DPI, grayscale, with consistent style.

Where to Sell Low-Content Books

Platform	Format	Notes
Amazon KDP	Paperback (POD)	Largest reach, evergreen traffic
Etsy	Digital downloads	Best for printable planners and bundles
Gumroad	Digital & bundles	Ideal for upselling multiple formats

Platform	Format	Notes
Teachers Pay Teachers	Worksheets	Great for education-focused workbooks
Payhip	Membership bundles	Sell access to a growing template library

Strategy Tip: Sell **digital versions on Etsy** and **print versions on KDP**—same content, two income streams.

Real-World Example: $5,200 in 90 Days With 3 Books

What Happened

Sam, a high school teacher, used ChatGPT and Canva to create:

A daily **affirmation journal** for teens

A 90-day **academic planner**

A math **puzzle workbook** for grades 3–5

She listed digital versions on Etsy and print editions via Amazon KDP. With simple ad spend and TikTok content showing her books in use, she hit:

$3,600 in KDP royalties

$1,600 from Etsy sales

2,800+ total units sold in 3 months

What We Learn From It

Sam didn't write a wordy book—she created **tools**. Her audience didn't care about prose—they wanted structure. By choosing functional formats and pairing AI with design templates, she built repeatable assets that compound over time.

Common Mistakes to Avoid

✖ Using overcomplicated layouts—simple = scalable

✖ Neglecting proofreading for prompts or headings

✖ Publishing without checking Amazon's bleed/margin requirements

✖ Creating "everything books" with no clear theme or audience

✖ Ignoring the value of good titles and covers (SEO + design matters)

Tactical Best Practices

Use consistent formatting—each page should feel familiar and clean

Optimize titles for keywords—e.g., "90-Day Productivity Planner for ADHD Entrepreneurs"

Design for black-and-white printing to lower KDP costs

Include sample pages in listings (on Etsy or Gumroad)

Add bonus content—digital downloads, printable stickers, or access to online tools

Test in bundles—sell 3-book sets for planners or journals to increase average order value

Checklist-Style Action Steps

Choose a niche that needs structured support (health, mindset, business, etc.)

Use AI to generate prompts, trackers, templates, or question sets

Design 1–3 simple layouts in Canva or BookBolt

Export interior as 6x9 PDF (KDP) or digital planner (Etsy)

Create matching cover designs and mockups

Upload to Amazon KDP with searchable titles and categories

Sell digital versions via Etsy, Gumroad, or TPT

Cross-promote via email, social reels, or bundles

Monitor reviews and requests to create spin-offs or variations

Think in Frameworks, Not Chapters

Low-content books are not about storytelling—they're about **empowering action**. The value is in the structure: the page that helps someone track their habit, plan their week, or teach a skill.

With AI, you can rapidly ideate, produce, and refine these assets—turning simple frameworks into real revenue. And because the content is evergreen, the sales don't stop when the launch ends.

Building an Author Brand With AI Support

In today's creator economy, publishing a book is no longer the finish line—it's the launchpad. Your real value isn't just the content you write, but the **credibility, visibility, and revenue streams you build around it**. And to compete in a saturated market, you need more than a single product—you need a brand.

That doesn't mean becoming an influencer or spending hours a day on social media. A modern author brand is about **consistency, trust, and a clear promise**—supported by intelligent systems that amplify your voice without burning you out.

This is where AI becomes a strategic advantage. Used well, it can help you scale your presence, refine your message, and deliver value across multiple channels—**without diluting your identity or losing human connection**.

In this section, we'll explore how to build a high-trust author brand powered by AI—from content production and marketing to positioning and backend monetization.

Why Branding Matters More Than Ever

There are millions of books on Amazon. Templates flood Etsy. Courses launch daily. The question isn't just, *"Is your product good?"* It's:

> *"Do I trust you?"*

> *"Do I understand what you stand for?"*

> *"Have I seen your name before?"*

> *"Do I believe your book will actually help me?"*

A strong author brand answers these questions before the reader ever clicks "Buy."

Done right, your brand becomes:

> A **reputation multiplier** (books, products, emails all reinforce your message)

> A **monetization engine** (you can launch new offers with minimal marketing)

A **filter** (your voice and values attract the right audience and repel the wrong one)

A **moat** (harder to copy than your products)

And with AI, you can build all of this **without hiring a team or spending thousands on freelancers.**

Elements of a Modern Author Brand

Your brand isn't your logo. It's the **strategic consistency** across your assets. It includes:

Element	Function
Author Voice	How you sound—confident, clear, grounded
Visual Identity	Colors, fonts, photography style (use Canva or Kittl)
Positioning	Who you help, what you help them achieve
Signature Framework	Your unique process or perspective (makes you memorable)
Platform Presence	Where you show up (Amazon, LinkedIn, Substack, Gumroad)
Product Ecosystem	Your books, templates, courses, services
Reputation Assets	Reviews, testimonials, interviews, partnerships

Branding is clarity. If your audience doesn't understand what you offer within 30 seconds, you don't have a brand—you have a product listing.

How AI Supports Each Stage of Brand Building

1. Clarifying Your Positioning

Use AI tools (like ChatGPT) to:

Refine your niche and reader promise

Generate positioning statements (e.g., "I help solopreneurs turn their knowledge into income-generating books and products")

Distill your unique angle (what makes your approach different)

Analyze competitor brands and identify whitespace

2. Generating Brand Language & Messaging

AI can help write:

Bio variations for different platforms

Taglines, mission statements, and about pages

Book blurbs and author intros

Pitch templates for podcasts, guest posts, and affiliate partnerships

Prompt Example:
"Write a professional author bio for a nonfiction writer helping small business owners build passive income with AI-powered tools."

3. Designing Visual Identity (Without Hiring a Designer)

Use tools like:

Canva Pro – Brand kits, social templates, media kits

Kittl – AI-assisted logo and typography creation

Khroma – AI-generated color palettes that match your brand mood

Looka – Logo and brand system generator

AI doesn't replace design—it gives you a **starting point** and fast iteration loop.

4. Content Repurposing at Scale

Your brand grows through consistent visibility, not one-off launches. AI can help:

Turn book chapters into newsletter issues

Turn interviews into quote graphics

Summarize longform content into LinkedIn posts

Repurpose templates or checklists into lead magnets

Best Tools:

ChatGPT + Claude – Writing, summarizing, adapting tone

Descript – Audio/video editing and transcription

Opus Clip – Turn long video clips into short social reels

Jasper – Branded social media content in your voice

Real-World Example: Branding With No Team

What Happened

Ethan published a Kindle book on **AI automation for service businesses**. Instead of going silent after launch, he used ChatGPT and Canva to build a minimalist, B2B-friendly author brand:

Created a consistent **black-and-white design aesthetic**

Used AI to draft weekly LinkedIn posts based on reader questions

Built a **Notion-based resource hub** for buyers (bonus from the book)

Repurposed book chapters into free email templates and calculators

Designed a one-page site with AI-generated blurbs, testimonials, and product links

Results in 90 days:

1,400 email subscribers (via in-book lead magnet and landing page)

4,800 followers on LinkedIn

$3,300 in additional digital product sales

2 speaking invitations from niche industry podcasts

What We Learn From It

Ethan didn't build a brand to "go viral." He built one to **be remembered, trusted, and easy to buy from.** AI helped him maintain visibility, consistency, and tone—without any staff or expensive contractors.

Common Mistakes to Avoid

✖ Inconsistent tone and visuals across platforms

✖ Relying too heavily on AI without human editing (bland = forgettable)

✖ Over-branding before clarity (don't design logos before messaging)

✖ Using AI to copy instead of clarify (authenticity always wins)

✖ Launching too many offers with no central identity

Tactical Best Practices

Pick 2–3 core platforms to show up consistently (Amazon, Substack, LinkedIn, etc.)

Create a brand voice guide using ChatGPT—how you speak, what you don't say

Use one visual identity across book covers, templates, social posts, and products

Build one high-trust lead magnet from your book to drive list growth

Focus on your reader's transformation, not your expertise

Reinforce your name on covers, URLs, email footers, and intros

Checklist-Style Action Steps

Define your niche, audience, and transformation in 1–2 sentences

Use ChatGPT to write your bio, elevator pitch, and tagline

Choose brand fonts, colors, and design elements in Canva

Build a lightweight landing page with email opt-in

Use AI to generate a weekly content system (1 post, 1 email, 1 CTA)

Reuse content across 2–3 platforms with minor edits

Add your personal domain to all products (e.g., yourbooksite.com)

Collect testimonials and reviews to reinforce trust

Use book back matter and email autoresponders to cross-sell other assets

Stay visible, but consistent—play the long game

You Are the Asset

In an AI-powered publishing economy, your greatest edge isn't volume. It's **voice**. The market is flooded with content—but starving for clarity, leadership, and trustworthy curation.

AI can help you **amplify and organize** what makes you valuable—but it's your perspective, not the algorithm, that builds a brand worth following.

CHAPTER 6

AI in E-Commerce & Print-on-Demand

POD Designs Generated by AI Art Tools

Print-on-demand (POD) remains one of the most accessible ways to turn creativity into income. Unlike traditional ecommerce, there's no inventory, no shipping, and no upfront production cost. You design once, upload to POD platforms, and earn royalties every time someone buys your design on a t-shirt, hoodie, tote bag, phone case, or mug.

What's new is how **AI art tools** have transformed this model. Instead of spending hours in Photoshop or Illustrator, you can now generate **unique, high-quality, commercially viable designs** in minutes with tools like MidJourney, DALL·E, Stable Diffusion, and Kittl. The challenge isn't creation anymore—it's knowing **what to make, how to optimize, and where to sell**.

This section walks you through using AI art to build a POD catalog that sells—not just clutters your hard drive with pretty images.

Why AI + POD Is a Powerful Income Stream

Zero upfront cost: No printing or stock to buy

Scalable catalog: Once uploaded, designs can sell for years

Global reach: POD platforms handle worldwide fulfillment

Fast iteration: AI lets you test 20 concepts in a day

Trend agility: You can respond to seasonal events, memes, or niche demands instantly

With the right prompts and positioning, AI allows solo creators to compete with design studios—without technical skills.

The POD Workflow: From Idea to Sale

Step 1: Research Niches and Trends

Don't design blindly. Use:

Etsy Search + Everbee Plugin – See what POD designs are trending

Merch Informer – Niche and keyword analysis for Amazon Merch

Pinterest – Visual style inspiration

Google Trends – Seasonality checks

Look for **evergreen niches** (pets, fitness, professions, hobbies) and **seasonal spikes** (holidays, graduations, new year resolutions).

Step 2: Generate Designs With AI Tools

Use AI to create original graphics based on prompts.

MidJourney – High-quality artistic styles (vector, retro, minimalist, cartoon)

DALL·E – Clean illustrations with strong object recognition

Stable Diffusion + ControlNet – Fine control over poses, shapes, and outputs

Kittl – Combine AI generation with text-based logos and layouts

Prompt Example for T-Shirt Vector:
"Flat vector illustration of a smiling golden retriever wearing sunglasses, bold outlines, pastel colors, minimalist style, centered composition, white background."

Export in **high resolution (300 DPI)** with transparent background for POD use.

Step 3: Clean and Adapt Designs

AI outputs often need light editing:

Canva – Background removal, resizing, mockups

Affinity Designer / Illustrator – Vectorize or refine shapes

Remove.bg – Fast background cleaning

Let's Enhance / Topaz AI – Upscale to print quality

Always test mockups on POD products—what looks good on screen may not translate well to fabric or mugs.

Step 4: Upload to POD Platforms

Choose platforms based on audience:

Redbubble – Trend-driven, broad global audience

TeeSpring – Focused on apparel, social selling integrations

Printful / Printify – POD fulfillment for your own Shopify or Etsy store

Amazon Merch on Demand – Massive audience, keyword-driven discoverability

Society6 – More design/art-driven customer base

Add **titles, tags, and descriptions** with SEO keywords. Example: "Funny Cat Yoga Shirt – Cartoon Vector Design – Cute Meditation Tee for Cat Lovers"

Step 5: Market & Cross-Sell

Don't rely solely on platform search. Share designs on:

Instagram / TikTok (show design-to-shirt process with AI behind the scenes)

Pinterest (pins linking back to Etsy store)

Email newsletter (feature seasonal drops)

Real-World Example: Scaling With AI Designs

What Happened
Amira, a college student, used MidJourney to create "quirky animal designs with funny slogans." She uploaded them to Redbubble and Merch by Amazon, starting with:

"Corgi in a Spacesuit"

"Sloth Doing Yoga"

"Panda Gamer with Headset"

She cleaned each design in Canva, applied to multiple products, and optimized listings with SEO tags.

Results in 6 months:

320+ designs uploaded

$2,800/month in POD royalties

Top 10 designs accounted for 70% of sales

Best-seller: "Sloth Yoga" tee, which spiked around New Year's resolution season

What We Learn From It

Amira didn't chase generic "cool" art—she combined **niche targeting (animals + humor)** with **AI-powered speed**. Upload volume plus clear positioning gave her a growing portfolio of evergreen earners.

Common Mistakes in AI-POD

✖ **Overly complex designs** that don't print well

✖ **Using copyrighted names or brands** in prompts (risk of takedown)

✖ **Ignoring POD platform guidelines** (many reject low-quality files)

✖ **No keyword optimization**—even great designs won't sell if they're invisible

✖ **Chasing only viral trends** without evergreen niches to stabilize revenue

Tactical Best Practices

Keep designs simple and bold (avoid tiny details that vanish on fabric)

Export transparent PNGs at 300 DPI for print quality

Test on multiple mockups before publishing (t-shirt, mug, tote bag)

Create bundles or themed collections (e.g., 5 pet designs, 10 motivational quotes)

Balance evergreen + seasonal designs for steady sales and spikes

Track your top 10 designs monthly and create variations to extend winners

Checklist-Style Action Steps

Research 3–5 profitable niches (pets, hobbies, professions, humor, etc.)

Use MidJourney/DALL·E to generate 20–30 design variations

Clean outputs in Canva/Illustrator and export at 300 DPI with transparent backgrounds

Upload designs to Redbubble, Merch by Amazon, Etsy, and/or Printify

Write SEO-optimized titles and tags for each design

Create collections (e.g., "Funny Yoga Animals" series)

Promote designs on Instagram, Pinterest, or TikTok with mockups

Track best sellers, create seasonal variants, and repeat

POD as a Scalable Asset Strategy

The strength of POD isn't one shirt—it's a **catalog**. With AI art, you can build that catalog 10x faster, covering multiple niches and testing designs at scale. Each upload is a lottery ticket—some flop, some sell a few copies, and a handful become long-term earners.

When combined with SEO, seasonal strategy, and bundles, POD becomes a **low-maintenance, compounding asset base**. Design once, upload once, and let sales roll in.

Shopify + AI-Driven Product Descriptions

Shopify has become the go-to platform for entrepreneurs building online stores. It offers global reach, seamless payment integration, and an ecosystem of apps that make running an e-commerce business accessible for solo founders and small teams. But success in Shopify doesn't come just from uploading products—it comes from **how you present them**.

One of the most overlooked leverage points is the **product description**. It's not filler—it's a **sales tool**. A great description improves SEO, builds trust, communicates value, and increases conversion rates. Yet most store owners either copy bland manufacturer text or write generic one-liners. That's where AI comes in.

With the right workflow, you can use AI to generate **high-converting, SEO-optimized, customer-centric product descriptions** at scale, freeing you to focus on marketing, fulfillment, and growth.

Why Product Descriptions Matter More Than You Think

Every product description serves two jobs:

For Humans (Conversion)

Clarify what the product is

Show benefits, not just features

Anticipate objections (size, durability, use case)

Create urgency or emotional appeal

For Algorithms (Discovery)

Include relevant keywords for search engines

Optimize for Google Shopping and Shopify's internal SEO

Use structured formatting for rich snippets (bullets, headings, etc.)

In other words, descriptions aren't about filling space—they're about **getting found and getting bought**.

How AI Enhances Shopify Product Pages

AI tools like **ChatGPT, Jasper, Copy.ai, or Writesonic** can help you:

Generate multiple description variations in seconds

Insert SEO keywords naturally

Adjust tone (playful, luxury, minimalist, corporate) for brand consistency

Localize content into multiple languages for international reach

Create short-form bullet highlights for mobile-first shoppers

A/B test different descriptions quickly

This isn't about letting AI write bland copy—it's about using AI as a **scalable copywriting assistant** while you provide strategy and final polish.

The AI-Driven Product Description Workflow

Step 1: Define Your Brand Voice

Before you start, clarify:

> Tone: Friendly, professional, luxury, minimalist?
>
> Audience: Who are you talking to (moms, students, athletes, business owners)?
>
> Promise: What does your store *stand for* (affordability, quality, lifestyle upgrade)?

Feed this into your AI tool as context.

Step 2: Research Keywords

Use **Google Keyword Planner, Ahrefs, or Ubersuggest** to identify:

> Core product keywords
>
> Long-tail terms ("eco-friendly yoga mat for travel")
>
> Search intent phrases ("best yoga mat for hot yoga")

Step 3: Generate Descriptions With AI

Prompt Example:
"Write a Shopify product description for a sustainable cork yoga mat. Use a warm, trustworthy tone. Highlight benefits for eco-conscious buyers, include SEO keywords like 'eco-friendly yoga mat' and 'non-slip cork surface,' and provide both a short bullet list and a 2-paragraph narrative."

Step 4: Edit for Clarity and Persuasion

Polish manually to:

Ensure factual accuracy (dimensions, shipping, materials)

Align tone with brand

Add urgency, social proof, or guarantees

Step 5: Structure for Conversion

Start with a **benefit-driven headline**

Add a **2–3 sentence intro** with emotional hook

Use **bullet points** for quick-scan features

End with a **call-to-action** (Buy now, Limited stock, etc.)

Example: AI-Powered Rewrite

Generic Manufacturer Text
"Cork yoga mat, size 72x24, 5mm thickness. Non-slip surface, made from natural cork and rubber."

AI-Enhanced Shopify Description
Headline:
🌿 Elevate Your Practice With a Sustainable Cork Yoga Mat

Body Copy:
Designed for eco-conscious yogis, this cork yoga mat combines sustainability with performance. The non-slip cork surface provides unmatched grip—even in hot yoga—while the 5mm cushioning supports joints through every pose. Crafted from natural cork and rubber, it's durable, portable, and gentle on the planet.

Bullet Highlights:

Eco-friendly, biodegradable materials

Non-slip cork surface for ultimate grip

Cushioned 5mm support for knees and joints

Lightweight yet durable for travel and studio use

Naturally antimicrobial and easy to clean

CTA:
Bring balance to your practice—and the planet. Order your eco-friendly cork yoga mat today.

Real-World Example: Boosting Sales With AI Copy

What Happened
A Shopify entrepreneur selling kitchen gadgets used AI to rewrite 120+ product descriptions. Each was tailored to:

Address a pain point (time-saving, easier cleanup, healthier cooking)

Include SEO keywords ("non-stick air fryer basket," "stainless steel garlic press")

Match brand voice (playful and modern)

After 60 days:

Organic search traffic increased by 42%

Add-to-cart rate rose by 18%

Time on page improved by 24 seconds (shoppers read more before bouncing)

What We Learn From It

Product descriptions weren't just words—they were levers for both discovery and conversion. AI provided the speed; editing and positioning provided the persuasion.

Common Mistakes to Avoid

✖ Publishing raw AI text without edits (feels robotic, kills trust)

✖ Keyword stuffing ("eco yoga mat, eco yoga mat, eco yoga mat")

✖ Using the same tone for every product (luxury skincare ≠ gym gear)

✖ Skipping mobile readability—most Shopify traffic is mobile-first

✖ Forgetting to update images and descriptions together

Tactical Best Practices

Batch-generate descriptions in AI, but edit each for uniqueness

Include benefits above features—always answer "why does this matter?"

Write for scanners: short paragraphs, bullets, headlines

Embed trust cues (sustainability claims, guarantees, customer-first language)

Localize descriptions for major regions (UK English, Spanish, etc.)

Test multiple variations—AI makes iteration cheap and fast

Checklist-Style Action Steps

Define your brand voice, audience, and positioning

Collect product details (size, materials, use cases)

Research SEO keywords for each product type

Generate multiple drafts using AI, tailored to tone + keywords

Edit for clarity, persuasion, and accuracy

Structure copy with headlines, bullets, and CTA

Upload to Shopify with clean formatting and images

Monitor add-to-cart and conversion rates

Iterate and optimize based on performance data

Descriptions as a Revenue Lever

Product descriptions aren't filler—they're revenue levers. With AI, you can turn bland listings into persuasive, search-friendly assets that work for you 24/7. One great description can multiply sales across thousands of visits. And when your store grows, AI ensures you can scale without losing consistency or burning out.

Automated Customer Service Chatbots

For small business owners and solo entrepreneurs, customer service is often a time sink. Answering the same questions—*"Where's my order?"*, *"How do I reset my password?"*, *"Do you offer refunds?"*—eats into hours that could be spent on growth. Yet ignoring these questions costs sales and damages trust.

This is where **AI-powered customer service chatbots** come in. Modern chatbots, unlike the clunky bots of five years ago, are conversational, context-aware, and capable of handling 60–80% of routine support without human intervention. For SMBs, this means **faster response times, lower overhead, and happier customers**.

When integrated properly, chatbots don't replace human care—they **filter, automate, and scale** so you can focus on higher-value tasks.

Why AI Chatbots Are a Game-Changer

Always-on availability: Customers get answers 24/7

Scalability: Handle thousands of chats simultaneously without hiring staff

Consistency: Every answer is accurate and on-brand

Revenue impact: Bots can upsell, cross-sell, or recover abandoned carts

Data insights: Track common issues, customer language, and pain points

For SMBs, the chatbot isn't just a support tool—it's a **sales multiplier and retention system**.

Types of Chatbots You Can Deploy

Type	Function	Best Use Case
FAQ Bots	Pre-programmed answers to common questions	Ecommerce, SaaS, services
Transactional Bots	Handle specific tasks (track order, book call, reset)	Shopify, booking platforms, B2B services
Conversational AI	Context-aware, learns from interactions	High-touch industries (finance, coaching)
Hybrid Bots	AI + live agent handoff	Best for small teams needing escalation

Best AI Tools for Customer Service Automation

Tool	Strengths	Ideal For
Tidio	Shopify/WordPress integration, ecommerce AI	Online stores
Intercom Fin	Deep AI knowledge base integration	SaaS, startups
Zendesk Answer Bot	Links to existing helpdesk content	Customer support-heavy SMBs
Drift	Conversational sales + lead qualification	B2B, consultants, high-ticket services
ManyChat	Social-first automation (FB, IG, WhatsApp)	Social sellers and creators
Claude or GPT via API	Custom-built assistants with your data	Tech-savvy founders, niche solutions

Pro Tip: Start with plug-and-play solutions like **Tidio** or **Intercom** before building custom GPT-powered bots.

The Automation Workflow: Building a Chatbot That Works

Step 1: Identify Core Customer Questions

List the top 10–20 recurring support queries:

> Shipping times

> Refunds and returns

> Product specs

> Account/password help

> Appointment bookings

Step 2: Build a Knowledge Base

Feed your chatbot FAQs, policy pages, and help docs. AI-powered bots can reference this dynamically.

Step 3: Configure Conversational Flow

Set up flows for:

> Greeting and brand tone

> Quick replies (buttons for "Track my order," "Refund policy")

> Escalation to human support if AI can't resolve

Step 4: Integrate With Platforms

Connect your bot to:

Shopify or WooCommerce for order tracking

Calendly or Acuity for booking

CRM/Helpdesk for escalation and ticketing

Email marketing tool for follow-up automations

Step 5: Train, Test, and Monitor

Run sample chats to refine tone

Track unanswered questions to expand training

Use analytics to see conversion impact

Real-World Example: Reducing Support Load by 70%

What Happened
A boutique ecommerce brand selling handmade jewelry was drowning in customer emails: order status, resizing questions, and refund policies.

They integrated **Tidio** with Shopify and trained the bot on their FAQ and return policy pages. The bot:

Answered 80% of shipping/order questions automatically

Collected emails from first-time visitors for discounts

Handed off only 20% of chats to the founder

Results in 90 days:

Support workload cut by 70%

$4,100 in additional sales from cart recovery sequences

Average response time dropped from 14 hours to instant

What We Learn From It
The chatbot wasn't just a cost saver—it became a revenue driver by nurturing leads and removing friction from purchases.

Common Mistakes to Avoid

❌ Over-automating—customers hate bots that refuse escalation

❌ Using generic AI with no brand training (leads to off-brand tone)

❌ Ignoring mobile-first design (most chats happen on phones)

❌ Not updating FAQs—outdated responses erode trust

❌ Treating bots only as cost-saving tools, not sales enhancers

Tactical Best Practices

Train bots on your own content (not generic AI data)

Blend quick-reply buttons + natural conversation

Add escalation triggers ("speak to human")

Keep tone human-like—friendly, empathetic, concise

Integrate order lookup for ecommerce to cut frustration

Use bots proactively—greet visitors, recover carts, recommend products

Checklist-Style Action Steps

Document top 20 customer questions/issues

Choose a chatbot platform (Tidio, Intercom, Zendesk, or custom GPT)

Train with your FAQ, policies, and knowledge base

Design conversational flows + escalation triggers

Connect bot to Shopify, booking apps, or CRM

Test across desktop and mobile

Monitor unanswered queries weekly and retrain

Use analytics to track conversions, deflections, and sales impact

Customer Service That Scales Without Staff

AI chatbots aren't here to replace human empathy—they're here to **filter, automate, and accelerate**. By handling repetitive queries instantly and reliably, they free you to focus on higher-value conversations, new product development, and strategic growth.

For small businesses, this is the closest thing to a **24/7 support team** without payroll. Get it right, and your chatbot won't just reduce costs—it will build trust, improve customer retention, and quietly increase your bottom line.

Niche Store Strategy for Long-Term Passive Sales

The ecommerce boom has made it easier than ever to open an online store—but also harder to stand out. General stores with "everything for everyone" rarely succeed anymore. Competing with Amazon or Walmart on breadth or price is a losing game.

The future of passive ecommerce lies in **niche stores**: focused, authority-driven shops that serve a specific audience with a curated set of products. When you combine a niche strategy with AI-powered tools for research, content, automation, and customer service, you create a store that can generate **steady, long-term sales with minimal ongoing effort**.

This section explores how to identify profitable niches, build brand authority, and set up systems that allow your store to run as a semi-passive income engine for years.

Why Niche Beats General Every Time

Trust factor: Customers buy from experts, not generalists. A store that only sells "eco-friendly pet products" feels more credible than one selling mugs, phone cases, and pet toys together.

SEO advantage: Ranking for niche keywords ("organic cat shampoo") is easier than competing for broad ones ("shampoo").

Content leverage: Blog posts, videos, and product descriptions all reinforce authority when tightly focused.

Loyalty loop: Niche customers come back because they feel understood—and they refer others in the same tribe.

Higher margins: Specialists can command premium pricing compared to general stores that compete on discounts.

Step 1: Choosing the Right Niche

A winning niche balances **passion, demand, and profitability**.

Ask yourself:

Does this audience have urgent or recurring needs?

Are there products that lend themselves to repeat purchases or upsells?

Is the market under-served (low competition but clear interest)?

Can I add authority with unique content, templates, or bundles?

Research Tools:

Google Trends: See interest over time

Etsy + Everbee: Identify trending keywords and products

Ahrefs/Ubersuggest: Keyword competition and traffic volume

Reddit/Quora: Find pain points in communities

Jungle Scout: Amazon product demand analysis

Examples of Evergreen Niches:

Remote work productivity gear

Pet wellness and eco-friendly accessories

Fitness recovery (foam rollers, massage tools, supplements)

DIY hobbies (gardening, woodworking, 3D printing)

Spirituality and mindfulness (journals, candles, crystals)

Step 2: Building the Store

For passive longevity, the store must feel **specialized, professional, and trustworthy**.

Platform Choices:

Shopify – Best for full-featured stores with apps and integrations

Etsy – Great for handmade, digital, or niche products

WooCommerce – Flexible if you already run a WordPress site

Core Store Elements:

Brand identity: Logo, niche-driven visuals, and consistent tone

Focused catalog: Start with 5–10 core products instead of 100+

Optimized descriptions: AI-generated and SEO-friendly (benefits first, then features)

Trust builders: Reviews, FAQs, guarantees, and clear shipping policies

Conversion boosters: Bundles, upsells, and subscription options

Step 3: Driving Sustainable Traffic

Your niche store doesn't need to rely solely on ads. Combine **evergreen SEO + niche authority content** to build compounding traffic.

Blog posts: "How to choose the best eco-friendly cat litter" → links directly to products

Video content: Quick TikTok or Instagram reels showing your products in use

Pinterest boards: Ideal for niches like decor, pets, hobbies, food, and wellness

Newsletters: Weekly tips, curated products, and stories from your niche

SEO optimization: Long-tail keywords that match buyer intent

AI can help generate blog drafts, social posts, product highlights, and even FAQs based on customer data.

Step 4: Automating Operations

To make your niche store passive, set up automation for:

Inventory & fulfillment: Use POD (Print-on-Demand) or dropshipping for hands-free logistics

Customer service: Deploy AI chatbots (Tidio, Intercom) for FAQs and order tracking

Email sequences: Automated welcome, abandoned cart recovery, and upsell flows

Social media scheduling: Batch content with Buffer, Hypefury, or Later

Analytics & reporting: Use Shopify apps or Google Analytics for automated dashboards

The goal: **Your store makes money even if you don't touch it for weeks.**

Real-World Example: Scaling a Niche Pet Wellness Store

What Happened
Maria launched a Shopify store focused on **eco-friendly pet care products**: compostable poop bags, organic shampoos, and non-toxic toys.

She used ChatGPT to:

Generate SEO-driven product descriptions

Create 20 blog posts for organic traffic

Write weekly newsletter intros with curated product links

She integrated Printful for POD packaging, Tidio for automated chat support, and Klaviyo for automated emails.

Results after 6 months:

$5,200/month in steady revenue

40% of sales from organic traffic

18% repeat customer rate

Workload: ~6 hours/week (content batching + monitoring)

What We Learn From It
Maria didn't chase volume. She chased **authority and alignment**. By going deep in a narrow market and automating everything she could, her store became a **semi-passive engine** rather than a job.

Common Mistakes to Avoid

✖ Starting too broad—"general gift store" = no authority

✖ Ignoring SEO and relying only on ads

✖ Uploading too many products at once (dilutes focus)

✖ Skipping brand consistency (random mix of product styles)

✖ Not collecting emails—your most reliable long-term channel

Tactical Best Practices

Pick a niche where you can add value beyond the product (education, guides, templates)

Launch with fewer products, but better presentation

Bundle and cross-sell to raise average order value

Leverage user-generated content (UGC) for social proof

Automate customer touchpoints for true passivity

Continuously mine your niche communities for new product ideas

Checklist-Style Action Steps

Research 3–5 niche markets using SEO + trend tools

Choose one with clear demand and low-to-medium competition

Set up Shopify (or Etsy/WooCommerce) with 5–10 curated products

Write AI-assisted, SEO-optimized product descriptions

Design blog and social content pillars around the niche

Automate fulfillment (POD or dropshipping)

Set up chatbots + email sequences for customer interactions

Monitor analytics monthly and double down on best-sellers

Niche Stores as Long-Term Digital Assets

A niche Shopify or POD store isn't just a side hustle—it's a **digital property**. Once it gains authority, traffic, and consistent sales, it becomes an asset you can scale, automate, or even sell.

In the age of AI, the biggest advantage isn't just faster product listings—it's **using AI to research, write, optimize, and automate** so your store keeps selling while you focus on strategy.

CHAPTER 7

AI in Education & Courses

Creating Online Courses With AI Co-Creators

The online course market has exploded into a multi-billion-dollar industry, but with that growth comes fierce competition. Today, anyone can record a video and call it a course. What separates the profitable, long-lasting courses from the forgettable ones is **clarity, structure, and authority**.

AI is not here to replace instructors—it's here to act as a **co-creator**. Used correctly, AI can help you plan, script, design, and market your course far faster than traditional methods, while you bring the expertise, stories, and trust your audience needs. The result? A course that feels polished, professional, and scalable—without months of development time.

Why Courses Are Still One of the Best Passive Income Vehicles

Evergreen demand: People will always pay to learn new skills, solve problems, or achieve personal growth.

High margins: Once built, courses can sell repeatedly with almost no delivery cost.

Scalability: Sell to 10 or 10,000 people with no extra workload.

Authority building: A strong course elevates your brand and opens doors to consulting, speaking, and partnerships.

Bundle potential: Courses can be packaged with books, templates, or memberships for recurring revenue.

When paired with AI, course creation goes from a 6-month slog to a 6-week system.

Step 1: Validate Your Course Idea

The biggest mistake in course creation is building a program nobody wants. Use AI for **market validation**:

> **ChatGPT or Claude**: Generate lists of common struggles in your niche.

> **Quora/Reddit**: Find recurring questions that signal demand.

> **Keyword tools (Ubersuggest, Ahrefs)**: Search for "how to..." queries with volume.

> **Survey tools**: Have AI draft surveys to send to your email list or community.

Prompt Example:
"List the top 10 struggles that beginner Etsy sellers face when trying to grow their shops into full-time income sources."

If your idea solves one of these struggles clearly and directly, you have a course worth building.

Step 2: Build a Strong Course Outline

AI excels at turning broad topics into structured learning paths. Start with your **transformation promise**:

> "By the end of this course, you will be able to [specific outcome]."

Then feed this into AI to generate module and lesson outlines.

Example Prompt:
"Create a 6-module course outline for beginners learning how to monetize a Shopify niche store. Each module should have 3–4 lessons and build toward a final project."

Polish the output with your expertise—swap generic lessons for real strategies, frameworks, or case studies.

Step 3: Script and Structure Content With AI

Use AI to:

Draft **lesson scripts** or speaking points.

Generate **examples, analogies, or case studies** to explain concepts.

Suggest **activities, quizzes, or reflection questions** for engagement.

Create **email drip sequences** to onboard students.

Important: Don't rely on AI word-for-word. Use it for scaffolding, then add your voice, stories, and credibility.

Step 4: Design Visuals and Materials

Professional courses need more than talking-head videos. AI design tools can speed up:

Slide decks: Canva Magic or Beautiful.ai for polished lesson slides.

Graphics and icons: MidJourney or DALL·E for unique visuals.

Handouts and workbooks: ChatGPT drafts exercises, Canva designs them.

Quizzes: AI generates question banks and answer explanations.

Pro Tip: Keep visuals **minimal and consistent**. Over-design distracts from learning.

Step 5: Record and Produce Efficiently

You don't need a Hollywood studio. Use:

Descript: Record, edit, and remove filler words automatically.

Loom: Quick screen-record lessons for software tutorials.

Camtasia: More advanced editing and annotations.

AI voice/narration (ElevenLabs): For intros, summaries, or alternative language versions.

Batch record 3–4 lessons at a time, then polish with AI editing tools.

Step 6: Choose the Right Platform

Platform	Best For	Notes
Teachable	Solopreneurs, business coaches	Clean UX, good for bundles
Thinkific	Structured courses, certifications	Quizzes, assignments, certificates
Kajabi	All-in-one marketing + courses	Pricey but powerful funnels
Gumroad/Payhip	Fast setup, indie creators	Great for smaller courses + low overhead
Udemy	Marketplace model	High traffic, but lower pricing control

For long-term passive income, host on your own **Teachable/Thinkific/Kajabi** site and cross-list a teaser or mini-course on **Udemy** for discoverability.

Step 7: Market and Monetize With AI

AI can streamline your entire course marketing funnel:

> **Landing pages**: Generate headlines, benefits, and CTAs with Copy.ai.

> **Email campaigns**: 5-part nurture sequences drafted by AI, then human-polished.

> **Ad copy**: Quick testing of multiple variations across FB/IG/LinkedIn.

> **Social snippets**: Repurpose course content into threads, carousels, or reels.

Bundle your course with **books, templates, or memberships** to increase perceived value and drive recurring revenue.

Real-World Example: $14,500 in 4 Months With AI-Supported Course

What Happened
James, a freelance marketer, created a course on **"AI for Small Business Marketing Automation."**

> Used ChatGPT to draft the outline and first-pass scripts.

> Designed slides in Canva and handouts in Notion.

> Recorded lessons with Loom + Descript editing.

> Launched on Thinkific, cross-promoted via Substack and LinkedIn.

> Created a 3-email AI-generated sales sequence.

Results after 4 months:

420 students enrolled at $49 each = $20,580 gross

$14,500 net after platform and ad costs

Course also drove 12 new consulting clients from student referrals

What We Learn From It
James didn't overcomplicate production. He used AI as scaffolding, positioned the course tightly, and layered backend offers. His course wasn't just income—it was a **client acquisition engine**.

Common Mistakes to Avoid

✖ Creating a course nobody asked for (no validation)

✖ Relying entirely on AI text (generic = forgettable)

✖ Overproduction before proof of concept (recording 20 hours, no sales)

✖ Neglecting marketing—courses don't sell themselves

✖ Pricing too low to be sustainable

Tactical Best Practices

Start with a **pilot course** (2–3 hours) before scaling to a signature program.

Use AI for **structure and support**, not as a replacement for your expertise.

Keep modules short (5–15 minutes per lesson).

Include at least one **interactive element** (quiz, workbook, challenge).

Upsell into coaching, templates, or memberships.

Continuously repurpose course material into content for traffic.

Checklist-Style Action Steps

Validate your course idea with community research and keywords

Define the transformation: "By the end, students will..."

Use AI to draft outline and scripts, then edit with your expertise

Design slides, handouts, and quizzes with Canva + ChatGPT

Record lessons in batches using Loom or Descript

Choose a hosting platform (Teachable, Thinkific, Kajabi, or Gumroad)

Set pricing and create a simple sales funnel

Launch with an email sequence and social snippets

Collect feedback and testimonials from first students

Iterate, improve, and scale marketing

Teaching as a Scalable Asset

Online courses aren't about perfection—they're about transformation. If your student can go from *stuck* to *successful* using your material, your course has value. AI helps you build that transformation faster and with more polish. You bring the expertise.

AI helps you scale it into a product that earns long after the work is done.

AI Tutors & Micro-Learning Apps

The global appetite for learning has shifted. Traditional online courses are still valuable, but today's learners increasingly prefer **bite-sized, on-demand learning experiences**. Instead of sitting through 40 hours of video, people want quick lessons they can apply immediately—in between meetings, commutes, or late-night study sessions.

This is where **AI tutors and micro-learning apps** step in. They combine the personalization of a one-on-one coach with the efficiency of short, focused lessons. For creators, this opens a powerful new income stream: **educational products that scale like software but feel personal like coaching**.

Why AI Tutors and Micro-Learning Work

Personalized feedback: AI can adapt to each learner's pace, gaps, and preferences.

Micro-format delivery: 2–5 minute lessons fit into modern attention spans.

Interactive learning: Instead of passively watching videos, users practice through chat, quizzes, or exercises.

Global accessibility: Learners can study anytime, anywhere, without time zones or scheduling.

Scalable income: Once built, an AI tutor can serve 10 or 10,000 learners with no extra cost.

This model blends the best of **edtech and coaching**, and it's already reshaping how professionals, students, and hobbyists upskill.

Types of AI Tutors and Micro-Learning Products

Product Type	Example Use Case	Tools You Can Use
AI Language Tutors	Practice Spanish, French, or English via chat	LangChain + GPT, or apps like Lingostar
Skill Micro-Courses	"5-Minute Marketing Tips" or "AI Prompts for Designers"	Teachable, Gumroad, or custom chatbots
Interactive Workbooks	Journals with AI-guided reflections	Notion + GPT integrations
Test Prep Bots	SAT, IELTS, or industry certification practice	ChatGPT fine-tuned with question banks
Corporate Training Apps	Compliance or product knowledge micro-lessons	Thinkific + AI plugins, Eduflow

Each of these can be packaged as **subscription apps, downloadable tools, or bundled products** within your ecosystem.

How to Build an AI Tutor or Micro-Learning App

Step 1: Define the Learning Outcome

What transformation does your learner want?

Example: "By the end of 30 days, users can hold a basic conversation in French" or "Marketers will master AI-powered ad copywriting."

Step 2: Chunk Content Into Micro-Lessons

Use AI to break content into **digestible, 3–5 minute modules**.

Each lesson = 1 concept + 1 example + 1 action step.

Avoid long lectures—focus on practical application.

Prompt Example:
"Break down a beginner's guide to content marketing into 20 micro-lessons. Each lesson should include a short explanation, an example, and a practice question."

Step 3: Choose Your Delivery Platform

No-Code Apps: Glide, Softr, Bubble → fast, app-like experiences

Chatbots: Typebot, Tidio, Landbot → interactive tutoring conversations

Learning Platforms: Thinkific, Teachable → add AI elements with Zapier/Make integrations

Custom API Builds: GPT + LangChain → advanced, personalized tutoring systems

Step 4: Add Personalization and Feedback

AI can quiz learners on each module.

Use memory functions to track learner progress.

Provide adaptive feedback: if a user fails, AI explains in simpler terms or gives extra examples.

Step 5: Monetize Smartly

Subscription model: $9–$49/month for continuous learning.

One-time payment: "Lifetime access to AI tutor + resources."

Bundles: Pair with a book, course, or templates for upsells.

Licensing: Sell corporate training modules to businesses.

Real-World Example: AI Tutor as a Side Income

What Happened
Lena, a language teacher, created an AI-powered **Spanish conversation tutor** using GPT via Typebot. The bot:

Delivered 30 days of 5-minute daily lessons.

Corrected grammar and suggested vocabulary in real time.

Integrated with email reminders and streak tracking.

She sold access on Gumroad for $29, promoted through TikTok language tips.

Results in 3 months:

820 paying users (~$23,780 revenue)

36% completed all 30 days (above industry average for online courses)

Teachers and coaches reached out for white-label licensing

What We Learn From It
By focusing on **convenience + personalization**, Lena created a micro-learning tool that felt intimate but scaled infinitely—something a human tutor couldn't replicate at the same price point.

Common Mistakes to Avoid

❌ Overloading lessons with too much information (micro ≠ mini-course)

❌ Not testing prompts—poorly tuned AI = frustrating learner experience

❌ Forgetting progression—random lessons don't build skills

❌ Relying on text only—add quizzes, examples, and interaction

❌ Pricing too low—undervalues the tool and reduces sustainability

Tactical Best Practices

Focus on one transformation—not everything your niche might need.

Keep lessons practical—1 idea, 1 example, 1 action.

Use AI memory to simulate continuity ("Last time we covered verbs...").

Include gamification—streaks, badges, or unlocks boost retention.

Test with beta users before launch to refine tone and flow.

Bundle micro-learning with larger offers—make it the "daily practice" complement to a book or course.

Checklist-Style Action Steps

Define a single, clear outcome your tutor/app delivers

Break content into 10–30 micro-lessons

Use AI to script explanations, examples, and quizzes

Choose a delivery method (no-code app, chatbot, learning platform)

Add personalization (progress tracking, adaptive feedback)

Decide on pricing (subscription, one-time, bundle, or license)

Launch to a small test audience and collect feedback

Optimize flow, tone, and lesson clarity before scaling

Promote via email, social content, or bundled with other products

Iterate monthly with user insights and trending needs

The Future of Learning Is Small, Smart, and Scalable

Long-form courses will always have a place, but the growth lies in **daily, bite-sized learning companions**. AI tutors and micro-learning apps turn your expertise into something **interactive, personalized, and infinitely scalable**. They don't just teach—they **coach, quiz, and encourage** learners in real time.

For creators, that means building once, refining often, and earning for years—while giving learners a tool that feels as close to a personal coach as technology allows.

Membership Community Models

In the past, creators relied on one-off product sales—books, courses, templates—to generate income. The problem with that model is simple: once the sale is done, the revenue stops. A **membership community** solves this by creating **recurring, predictable income** while deepening customer loyalty.

AI makes this model even more powerful. Instead of struggling to keep up with constant content demands, you can use AI to support content creation, moderation, personalization, and engagement— allowing you to focus on leadership and vision. The result is a **scalable, sustainable business model** where members pay for access, connection, and transformation.

Why Membership Models Work

Recurring revenue: Monthly or yearly subscriptions mean predictable cash flow.

Stronger community ties: Members feel they belong to something bigger.

Higher retention: Ongoing value keeps customers engaged long-term.

Authority building: Running a community establishes you as the go-to leader in your niche.

Upsell opportunities: Communities are the best place to introduce higher-ticket offers (coaching, masterminds, premium services).

Memberships thrive not on how much content you deliver, but on **the outcomes and relationships you create**.

Common Membership Models

Model	Description	Example Niches
Content Library	Access to exclusive articles, templates, or tools	AI prompts, business templates, design packs
Cohort-Based Learning	Members progress through content together in cycles	Fitness programs, language learning
Community + Coaching	Access to group Q&A, live sessions, and peer support	Consulting, creative industries
Premium Newsletter	Paywalled email series with deeper insights	Industry trends, investment strategies
Hybrid Model	Mix of content, community, and events	Online academies, creator collectives

Platforms to Host Memberships

Platform	Best For	Notes
Circle	All-in-one: community, events, courses	Clean UX, great for paid memberships
Mighty Networks	Community-driven memberships	Includes courses, mobile app
Kajabi	Courses + memberships + funnels	High price but all-in-one system
Patreon	Tiered membership support for creators	Better for content-first communities

Platform	Best For	Notes
Discord/Slack	Casual, chat-based communities	Use AI bots for moderation and engagement
Substack	Premium newsletters with subscriber chat	Best for writing-driven memberships

How AI Supercharges Membership Communities

Content creation: AI drafts discussion prompts, lesson summaries, or resource guides.

Personalization: Chatbots answer FAQs, recommend resources, or guide new members.

Moderation: AI filters spam, flags inappropriate content, and ensures quality control.

Engagement: AI can suggest relevant discussion threads or connect members with similar interests.

Analytics: AI tools track engagement trends and suggest retention strategies.

Example Prompt:
"Generate 10 weekly discussion prompts for a membership community of small business owners learning AI automation. Each should encourage peer sharing and practical tips."

Real-World Example: $12,000/Month From a Hybrid Membership

What Happened
Carla, a productivity coach, launched a **Circle-based membership** for remote workers. Her offer included:

Weekly AI-assisted content drops (templates + summaries)

A live monthly coaching call

A supportive community forum with accountability threads

Exclusive discounts on her other products

She priced at $29/month with ~500 members in 8 months. AI supported her by:

Drafting weekly email recaps

Generating challenge prompts ("3-Day Focus Reset")

Auto-summarizing live session transcripts into PDFs

Results:

~$12,000/month in recurring revenue

40% of members stayed past 6 months

Increased course and coaching sales via upsells

What We Learn From It
Carla wasn't just selling access to content—she was selling **connection + accountability**. AI handled the repetitive work so she could stay focused on relationships.

Common Mistakes to Avoid

✖ Overpromising content (burnout follows quickly).

✖ Ignoring onboarding—members leave if they don't know where to start.

✖ Letting discussions die—communities need active facilitation.

✖ Focusing only on volume—quality of members matters more than quantity.

✖ Treating memberships as "set and forget"—they require ongoing leadership.

Tactical Best Practices

Start with a pilot group (20–50 members) before scaling.

Price based on transformation, not quantity of content.

Automate onboarding with AI (welcome guides, FAQs, role assignment).

Mix evergreen and live elements (library + calls + challenges).

Reward engagement (badges, shout-outs, gamified streaks).

Offer tiers—low-cost access tier + premium mastermind level.

Collect testimonials constantly to fuel retention and marketing.

Checklist-Style Action Steps

Define your community's core promise ("By joining, members will…")

Choose a platform (Circle, Mighty Networks, Patreon, etc.)

Decide on your model (content, coaching, newsletter, hybrid)

Use AI to create starter resources and engagement prompts

Build an onboarding sequence with clear first steps

Launch with a beta group to refine pricing and content flow

Add AI moderation or chatbots for scale and safety

Offer upsells (courses, coaching, templates) inside the community

Track churn and engagement weekly, adjust as needed

Celebrate milestones—community health drives retention

Memberships as Digital Ecosystems

A membership isn't just a revenue model—it's a **relationship engine**. Your role is to lead, guide, and inspire. AI helps by keeping content fresh, conversations flowing, and operations smooth. When done right, your membership community becomes more than a product—it becomes the hub of your entire business.

Upselling Consulting From Passive Products

Passive income products—books, courses, templates, and AI-powered apps—are powerful assets. They create leverage, authority, and recurring sales. But the truth is this: **the highest-value opportunities often come after the sale**.

When someone buys your passive product, they're not just purchasing information—they're signaling trust and interest in your expertise. That moment creates a natural opening for **consulting and advisory upsells**, where you trade specialized access to your brain (at a premium) instead of broad access to your content (at scale).

Done strategically, passive products become the **front door** to consulting engagements—where hourly rates, retainers, or project fees can dwarf digital product revenue.

Why Consulting Is the Natural Upsell

Authority established: If they bought your book or course, they already see you as credible.

Problem still unsolved: Many customers realize they'd rather pay you to guide them directly.

High willingness to pay: Businesses and professionals will spend $2,000–$20,000+ for tailored help.

Efficiency: You don't need to chase cold leads—your products warm them for you.

Scalability in tiers: Passive products serve the many; consulting serves the few at premium rates.

Where to Insert Consulting Upsells

Books and eBooks

Back matter CTA: "Need hands-on help implementing this system? Visit [yourURL]."

Bonus resource opt-in leading to a consulting pitch.

Online Courses

Offer a premium package: course + 3 consulting calls.

Mid-course check-in email upselling personalized coaching.

Templates & Digital Assets

Add a callout: "Want this customized for your business? Book a consult."

Offer setup packages alongside your template packs.

Membership Communities

Host a "Pro Tier" that includes monthly strategy calls.

Position 1:1 consulting as the logical next step for advanced members.

Webinars and Workshops

Deliver value live, then pitch consulting as the tailored solution.

Offer a "done-with-you" upgrade for attendees.

Structuring Consulting Offers

Not all consulting needs to be long-term. Create **tiered offers** that match different buyer levels:

Offer Type	Description	Price Range (Typical)
Clarity Call	60–90 minute one-off strategy session	$250–$1,000
Implementation Package	Short project with deliverables	$2,000–$7,500
Retainer	Ongoing advisory or coaching	$1,500–$10,000/month
VIP Day/Weekend	Intensive, focused work with fast outcome	$3,000–$15,000

The key is making the **path from passive → consulting frictionless**. Customers should see consulting as the "obvious next step" if they want faster or deeper results.

How AI Supports Consulting Upsells

Lead identification: AI can segment product buyers by engagement, signaling who's most likely to upgrade.

Automated emails: Personalized follow-ups inviting buyers to strategy sessions.

Proposal writing: AI drafts clear consulting proposals and contracts.

Prep materials: Summarize client submissions into pre-consultation briefs.

Scalable delivery: Use AI templates, reports, or dashboards to save hours of manual prep.

Real-World Example: $8,000 From a $29 eBook

What Happened
Mark, a cybersecurity consultant, self-published an eBook on **"AI Risks for Small Businesses."** In the back of the book, he added a link to book a free 20-minute discovery call.

Within 3 months:

640 eBook sales ($18,560 revenue).

14 discovery calls → 6 consulting clients.

Consulting contracts ranged from $2,500 to $6,000.

Total consulting revenue: $38,000.

What We Learn From It
The eBook wasn't just a product—it was a **sales funnel disguised as authority**. Mark positioned himself as the trusted expert, then made consulting the natural upgrade path.

Common Mistakes to Avoid

✖ Hiding consulting offers too deep in your product (people won't dig).

✖ Positioning consulting as "extra help" instead of **premium transformation**.

✖ Offering the same consulting service to everyone—tiered options convert better.

✖ Using generic CTAs—vague invites don't convert.

✖ Over-committing consulting hours without boundaries (burnout risk).

Tactical Best Practices

Always include a consulting CTA in books, courses, templates, and memberships.

Frame consulting as the "fast track" to implementation.

Automate discovery call booking with tools like Calendly + Zapier.

Pre-qualify leads (questionnaires to filter tire-kickers).

Use client testimonials in consulting upsell pitches.

Limit consulting slots to increase scarcity and protect your time.

Checklist-Style Action Steps

Define 2–3 consulting offers (clarity call, package, retainer).

Add consulting CTAs to all passive products (books, courses, templates).

Set up an automated booking funnel (Calendly + email follow-ups).

Use AI to draft proposals, onboarding docs, and prep materials.

Create upsell emails triggered by product purchases.

Promote "done-with-you" or "VIP Day" upgrades for power users.

Track conversions and adjust messaging based on feedback.

Protect your time—decide max consulting hours/month.

Passive Products as Your Consulting Funnel

Your passive products are more than revenue—they're **lead generators**. Every book, template, or course is proof of expertise. By positioning consulting as the "premium path" for faster, deeper results, you transform one-time buyers into high-value clients.

AI ensures you can manage the funnel without drowning in admin—automating follow-ups, proposals, and prep. That means you can scale **both your passive income and your consulting practice** without splitting yourself in two.

CHAPTER 8

Scaling & Automating Marketing with AI

AI SEO Research and Automated Blog Clusters

Search engine optimization (SEO) is still one of the most reliable ways to build **evergreen, compounding traffic**—the kind that drives passive sales long after your marketing campaigns end. But doing SEO the traditional way is slow: hours of keyword research, competitor analysis, and content planning before you even start writing.

AI changes this completely. With the right workflow, you can go from **idea → keyword map → content outline → blog cluster** in hours, not weeks. That means faster visibility, more organic leads, and an automated system for ranking in Google while you focus on monetization.

Why Blog Clusters Beat Random Posts

Most websites fail at SEO because they publish scattered articles without strategy. A **blog cluster** solves this by organizing content around a **core topic (pillar)** with supporting articles that interlink.

For example:

Pillar Topic: "AI Tools for Small Businesses"

Cluster Posts:

"Top AI Chatbots for Customer Support"

"How to Automate Bookkeeping With AI"

"AI Tools for Social Media Scheduling"

"Pros and Cons of AI in SMB Operations"

Google sees the interlinking structure as authority on the subject, rewarding you with higher rankings and faster organic growth.

How AI Streamlines SEO Research

AI tools can now handle the heavy lifting:

Keyword Research: Generate long-tail keyword lists with search intent classification.

Competitor Analysis: Summarize top-ranking posts and find content gaps.

Topic Clustering: Map out related keywords and queries into groups.

Content Briefs: Draft outlines optimized for readability, depth, and SEO best practices.

SERP Simulation: Predict how your content would rank for specific terms.

Tools You Can Use:

ChatGPT / Claude: Research and cluster keywords, draft outlines.

Surfer SEO: On-page optimization + keyword density recommendations.

Ahrefs / SEMrush: Data-driven keyword volumes and competition scores.

NeuronWriter / Frase: AI-assisted content briefs and SERP analysis.

Workflow: AI-Powered SEO Blog Cluster

Step 1: Define Your Pillar Topic

Example: "AI for Passive Income."

Step 2: Generate Cluster Keywords

Prompt:
"List 20 long-tail keywords related to 'AI for passive income,' grouped by user intent (informational, transactional, navigational)."

AI output might include:

> Informational: "How to make passive income with AI tools," "AI side hustles 2025"

> Transactional: "Best AI course for entrepreneurs," "AI tools subscription for business owners"

> Navigational: "Teachable AI course review," "Jasper AI pricing"

Step 3: Build a Blog Cluster Map

> Pillar Post: "Complete Guide to Passive Income With AI"

> Cluster Posts:

>> "10 AI Tools That Create Income Streams in 2025"

>> "Case Study: How I Automated My Shopify Store With AI"

>> "Best AI Apps for Digital Product Creators"

>> "AI Risks: What to Avoid When Building Automated Income"

Step 4: Create Content Briefs

Ask AI:
"Create a detailed blog outline for the keyword 'Best AI apps for digital product creators.' Include H2/H3 headings, FAQs, and a suggested meta description."

Step 5: Draft and Optimize

Use AI for first drafts.

Edit manually for brand voice, accuracy, and examples.

Run through Surfer SEO or Frase for keyword density and readability.

Step 6: Automate Internal Linking

Set rules in your CMS (WordPress, Webflow, Ghost) or use plugins like Link Whisper to auto-suggest cluster links.

Real-World Example: 10x Organic Traffic in 6 Months

What Happened
A solopreneur running a digital template store built an AI-driven blog cluster around "Notion productivity systems."

Pillar: "Ultimate Guide to Notion for Productivity"

Clusters: habit trackers, team dashboards, client portals, monetizing Notion templates.

Used ChatGPT to generate outlines and FAQs, then edited for depth.

Scheduled 3 posts per week for 3 months with WordPress automation.

Results:

Organic traffic grew from 1,200 to 12,000 visits/month.

Email list tripled (lead magnets in each post).

Template sales increased by 42%, adding $2,900 MRR.

What We Learn From It
The structured blog cluster strategy signaled topical authority to Google. AI accelerated production, but human editing ensured depth and trust.

Common Mistakes to Avoid

✖ Publishing raw AI text with no editing (Google penalizes low-quality content).

✖ Mixing unrelated topics in one blog (dilutes topical authority).

✖ Skipping interlinking between posts (clusters won't work without it).

✖ Ignoring search intent (ranking for keywords buyers never use).

✖ Focusing only on volume instead of **quality + relevance**.

Tactical Best Practices

Target long-tail keywords first—they're easier to rank and convert better.

Use FAQ sections with schema markup for featured snippets.

Refresh content every 6–12 months—AI can suggest updates fast.

Write pillar posts >2,500 words and clusters 1,000–1,500 words.

Batch content production—generate 10 outlines in AI, then edit weekly.

Always include CTAs to passive products (ebooks, templates, courses).

Checklist-Style Action Steps

Pick 1 pillar topic tied to your products.

Use AI to generate 20–50 supporting cluster keywords.

Map them into a blog cluster structure (pillar + supporting posts).

Create AI-assisted outlines with H2/H3s and FAQs.

Draft and edit 2–3 posts per week until the cluster is complete.

Optimize with Surfer SEO or Frase for keyword placement.

Automate interlinking and add product CTAs.

Monitor Google Search Console for rankings and update quarterly.

Blog Clusters as SEO Assets

Every well-structured cluster is more than just a set of blog posts—it's a **traffic engine**. With AI accelerating research and drafting, you can build topical authority in weeks instead of years. And once those posts rank, they continue sending leads and customers into your funnel—feeding your books, templates, courses, or consulting offers.

Social Media Auto-Content Engines

Social media is a double-edged sword for creators and entrepreneurs. On one hand, it's the fastest way to reach audiences, test ideas, and build authority. On the other, it's a relentless machine that demands constant posting—daily or even multiple times per day. For many small business owners, this grind becomes unsustainable.

That's why building a **social media auto-content engine** is one of the smartest investments for long-term growth. By combining AI writing, design, scheduling, and repurposing tools, you can create a **system that feeds your social channels automatically**—turning content into an evergreen traffic driver for your products and brand.

Why You Need an Auto-Content Engine

Consistency wins: Algorithms reward steady posting, not random bursts.

Authority through volume: The more high-quality posts you share, the more visible and trusted you become.

Leverage: One blog, podcast, or video can be repurposed into 20+ posts.

Time freedom: Automating ideation, formatting, and scheduling frees you to focus on business growth.

Scalable marketing: Even small teams (or solos) can look like a media company.

The AI-Powered Auto-Content Workflow

Step 1: Content Pillars

Define 3–5 recurring themes that align with your products and audience.

Examples:

"AI Tools for Business Growth"

"Passive Income Strategies"

"Customer Success Stories"

"Quick How-Tos"

Feed these into AI tools to generate endless variations.

Step 2: Ideation at Scale

Prompt AI to brainstorm dozens of post ideas per pillar.

Example Prompt:
"Generate 30 social media post ideas on the topic of 'AI automation for small businesses.' Include tips, myths, case studies, and questions for engagement."

Step 3: Content Drafting

Use AI to create first drafts in different formats:

Tweets/threads

LinkedIn posts

Instagram captions

TikTok/Reel scripts

Then edit for voice and clarity.

Step 4: Visual Creation

AI tools like **Canva Magic Design**, **Kittl**, or **DALL·E** can auto-generate:

Quote graphics

Carousel slides

Infographics

Meme-style images

Pair visuals with AI-generated copy for multi-platform impact.

Step 5: Repurposing Long-Form Content

One blog post or video can fuel weeks of posts:

Blog → Twitter thread → LinkedIn carousel → Instagram Reel script → Pinterest infographic.

Use **OpusClip** or **Descript** to turn long videos into short clips.

Step 6: Scheduling & Automation

Use scheduling tools to distribute automatically:

Buffer / Later – Multi-platform scheduling.

Hypefury – Twitter/X auto-threads and engagement.

Publer – Recycle evergreen posts.

Zapier/Make – Automate reposting or distribution.

Set up a content calendar once, then let automation drip-feed posts for weeks.

Real-World Example: 10x Audience Growth With Auto-Content

What Happened
An AI consultant built a content engine from her weekly newsletter. Each issue became:

1 LinkedIn article

3 short Twitter/X threads

2 Instagram carousels (using Canva templates)

5 quick video clips via OpusClip

She scheduled everything in Buffer.

Results after 90 days:

LinkedIn followers: 2,800 → 11,200

Newsletter list: 3,400 new subscribers

Book sales tripled due to consistent exposure

Time invested: ~2 hours per week

What We Learn From It
She didn't "do more." She **did once, multiplied with AI, and automated distribution**. The engine made her brand visible daily without draining her.

Common Mistakes to Avoid

✖ Treating AI drafts as final copy—bland posts won't cut through noise.

✖ Overposting identical content on every platform (audiences expect nuance).

✖ Skipping engagement—automation doesn't mean ignoring replies.

✖ Using AI images with text overlays (most platforms deprioritize).

✖ Focusing only on reach without linking back to your core products.

Tactical Best Practices

Batch-create 2–4 weeks of content at a time.

Keep formats native (threads for X, carousels for LinkedIn/IG, reels for TikTok).

Add engagement hooks: questions, polls, or CTAs.

Rotate evergreen posts every 3–6 months for compounding exposure.

Track performance—double down on formats that convert (not just go viral).

Always link back to an asset: book, course, template, or newsletter.

Checklist-Style Action Steps

Define 3–5 content pillars aligned with your products.

Use AI to brainstorm 50+ post ideas per pillar.

Draft posts in multiple formats (threads, carousels, reels).

Design visuals with Canva/DALL·E for each pillar.

Repurpose blogs, newsletters, or videos into micro-posts.

Load content into Buffer, Hypefury, or Later for automated scheduling.

Engage with replies/comments daily to build relationships.

Review analytics monthly and optimize for top-performing posts.

Social Engines as Business Assets

A social auto-content engine isn't about "posting more." It's about creating a **repeatable pipeline** where your expertise, once published, multiplies across channels automatically. AI handles the heavy lifting; you handle the authenticity and engagement.

When paired with strong CTAs, your auto-content engine doesn't just grow followers—it consistently drives them toward your **books, courses, memberships, and consulting offers**.

AI-Enhanced Ad Campaigns and Targeting

Paid advertising has always been about precision—putting the right message in front of the right audience at the right time. But in traditional ad campaigns, small business owners often waste money guessing which creative, audience, or platform will perform best. Budgets get burned fast.

AI flips the script. With intelligent targeting, predictive analytics, and automated creative testing, AI tools allow even small teams to run **enterprise-level ad campaigns** with far less trial and error. The result: better ROI, lower customer acquisition costs, and ads that feel personalized rather than generic.

Why AI Is Reshaping Digital Advertising

Smarter targeting: AI platforms analyze behavioral, contextual, and purchase data to identify high-probability buyers.

Dynamic creative optimization (DCO): Ads adjust text, visuals, or CTAs in real time based on user profiles.

Faster testing: AI can run thousands of micro-tests simultaneously, finding winners quickly.

Budget efficiency: Automated bidding adjusts spend toward ads that convert.

Scalability: Small budgets can compete with bigger players by using intelligence, not brute force.

Instead of spending weeks manually testing copy, AI lets you deploy optimized campaigns in hours.

AI Tools for Smarter Ad Campaigns

Tool	Strengths	Platforms Covered
Facebook Advantage+	Automates targeting + creative optimization	Facebook, Instagram
Google Performance Max	AI-driven across Search, YouTube, Display	Google Ads ecosystem
Jasper Ads	Generates multiple ad copy variations fast	FB/IG/Google/LinkedIn
Albert AI	Fully autonomous cross-channel ad optimization	Multichannel (search, social, display)
Phrasee	AI-generated ad subject lines + CTAs	Email + paid ads
AdCreative.ai	Auto-generates ad visuals + text pairings	FB/IG/LinkedIn/Google Display

Workflow: Building AI-Powered Ad Campaigns

Step 1: Define Your Objective

Awareness → broad targeting, storytelling ads

Leads → lead-gen forms, webinars, low-ticket entry points

Sales → retargeting, testimonials, product demos

Step 2: Audience Research

Use AI to analyze your ideal customers:

   Interests, pain points, and motivations

   Lookalike audiences based on existing buyers

   Predictive segments (e.g., "users likely to churn" or "repeat
      purchasers")

Prompt Example:
"Generate 5 customer personas for a course teaching solopreneurs
how to create passive income with AI. Include goals, frustrations,
and what type of ad messaging would appeal most."

Step 3: Generate Creative Variations

AI can create:

   10+ headlines targeting different emotions (fear, aspiration,
      curiosity)

   Multiple ad copy blocks with different value propositions

   Image variations (Canva + AdCreative.ai)

   Video scripts for 15–30 second ads

Step 4: Deploy Dynamic Creative

Upload all variations into platforms like **Meta Advantage+** or
Google Performance Max. AI automatically tests combinations and
optimizes in real time.

Step 5: Monitor and Refine

Track CTR, CPC, and conversion rates weekly

Use AI-driven reports (e.g., Google Analytics 4 insights) to spot trends

Recycle winning creatives across channels, kill losers early

Real-World Example: Cutting CAC in Half

What Happened
A fitness coach selling an **AI-personalized nutrition app** used AdCreative.ai + Facebook Advantage+.

AI generated 20 ad visuals and 15 copy variations.

Audiences were segmented into: busy parents, athletes, and young professionals.

Dynamic creative testing auto-optimized copy/images to each audience.

Results after 60 days:

CAC dropped from $22 to $10.40.

Conversions doubled with the same ad spend.

70% of sales came from two "surprise" winning ad combos AI surfaced.

What We Learn From It
AI found patterns the coach wouldn't have guessed—like parents responding best to "5-minute healthy meal hacks" visuals. Without AI, these insights would've cost months of wasted spend.

Common Mistakes to Avoid

✖ Running one ad set at a time instead of feeding AI multiple variations.

✖ Ignoring creative—AI can optimize only if you supply strong inputs.

✖ Over-targeting small audiences (let AI explore broader pools first).

✖ Failing to connect ads to optimized landing pages (ads can't fix poor websites).

✖ Relying only on CTR—focus on **conversion ROI**, not just clicks.

Tactical Best Practices

Feed AI 5–10 creatives per campaign to maximize optimization.

Match copy tone to funnel stage (educational → trust; retargeting → urgency).

Test short-form video—AI-optimized 15-second clips convert best on social.

Always install pixels (Meta Pixel, GA4) for retargeting and attribution.

Run smaller daily budgets across multiple audiences—let AI reallocate spend.

Pair ads with email funnels for long-tail nurturing.

Checklist-Style Action Steps

Define campaign objective (awareness, leads, or sales).

Use AI to generate customer personas and pain points.

Draft 10+ copy variations and 5+ visual assets with AI tools.

Deploy via Advantage+ (FB/IG) or Performance Max (Google).

Set budget with broad targeting and let AI optimize.

Monitor CPC, CTR, and conversion weekly.

Kill underperformers, scale winners.

Build retargeting audiences from site visitors and email subscribers.

Refresh creatives monthly to avoid ad fatigue.

Ads That Work While You Sleep

AI ad engines don't just save time—they **multiply your marketing intelligence**. By automating testing, targeting, and creative optimization, you can run campaigns that improve themselves over time. That means less wasted budget, more conversions, and ads that keep working while you focus on building assets.

Influencer Seeding & Viral Loop Strategies

One of the fastest ways to accelerate visibility for your AI-powered products—whether it's a book, course, template, or tool—is through **influencer seeding**. Instead of pouring money into broad ads, you strategically place your product in the hands of people who already command attention in your niche. When paired with **viral loop mechanics**, this creates a system where every customer or influencer touchpoint drives more growth without constant reinvestment.

What Is Influencer Seeding?

Influencer seeding is the process of **giving your product to key creators, experts, or community leaders** in exchange for exposure, reviews, or word-of-mouth. Unlike traditional influencer marketing (paid sponsorships), seeding is about **organic alignment**: find people who genuinely benefit from your product and let them amplify it to their followers.

This works because:

Audiences trust peer recommendations more than ads.

Micro-influencers often outperform celebrity endorsements.

Strategic gifting creates goodwill and authentic testimonials.

The Viral Loop Effect

A viral loop occurs when **using your product naturally leads to sharing it**, bringing in new users who repeat the cycle.

Examples in the passive income and AI space:

Books: Readers who unlock a bonus resource get a referral link or discount to share.

Courses: Students get affiliate codes to invite friends.

Apps/Tools: Free credits or templates are unlocked when a user shares with others.

Communities: Members earn rewards for inviting peers.

The key is to **embed sharing incentives into the product experience itself**, rather than relying on one-off campaigns.

Building Your Influencer Seeding Strategy

Identify Influencers by Niche

Use tools like SparkToro, HypeAuditor, or simple hashtag searches.

Focus on micro-influencers (5K–50K followers) with engaged audiences.

Create Shareable Assets

Offer a free copy of your book, course access, or template bundle.

Personalize with notes: "Thought this would help your community."

Automate Outreach

Draft AI-personalized pitches that feel human, not spammy.

Example: "I saw your thread on [topic]. I created a resource that might fit—want me to send it?"

Track Engagement

Use referral links or custom codes to measure ROI.

Identify which influencers drive actual sales vs. vanity traffic.

Viral Loop Triggers You Can Add Today

Referral discounts: "Give $10, Get $10" on digital products.

Gamified streaks: Share daily progress in exchange for rewards.

Exclusive unlocks: Bonus lessons, templates, or features when inviting friends.

Affiliate models: Offer influencers revenue share for every sale.

Real-World Example: Template Pack Seeding

What Happened
A designer selling AI-enhanced Canva templates gifted her product to 40 mid-level Instagram influencers in the creative entrepreneur space.

18 of them shared the templates in stories.

She layered in a referral link that gave influencers 30% of sales.

Customers who bought also got a "share to unlock 5 bonus templates" CTA.

Results in 60 days:

1,200+ new customers

$19,600 in revenue

4,500 new email subscribers

Zero ad spend—growth came entirely from seeding + viral loop mechanics

What We Learn From It
She didn't chase big-name influencers or massive ad budgets. She built a **growth flywheel**: seed → share → reward → repeat.

Common Mistakes to Avoid

✖ Sending products without clear value alignment (irrelevant audiences won't convert).

✖ Treating influencer seeding like a one-off stunt instead of a system.

✖ Ignoring attribution—without tracking links, you won't know what worked.

✖ Over-relying on one influencer—build a portfolio of promoters.

✖ Forgetting to reward existing customers—viral loops work best when everyone shares.

Tactical Best Practices

Start small: target 20–30 micro-influencers at first.

Make it personal: AI can draft intros, but always humanize.

Embed virality into products: don't bolt it on later.

Use incentives that align with your niche (discounts, extra content, community perks).

Measure impact: track which influencers and referral triggers drive ROI.

Stack channels: combine seeding with social auto-engines and SEO clusters for compounding exposure.

Checklist-Style Action Steps

Identify 20–50 micro-influencers in your niche.

Create share-ready versions of your product (books, templates, course access).

Draft AI-assisted outreach messages with personal context.

Add referral links or discount codes to track results.

Build viral mechanics into your product (bonus unlocks, referral credits).

Track conversions and double down on top influencers.

Incentivize existing customers to share, not just influencers.

Refresh offers quarterly to keep loops alive.

Conclusion

The future of passive income is not about working harder—it's about building systems that multiply your reach. Influencer seeding and viral loop strategies are two of the most effective multipliers available. Instead of chasing every follower one by one, you plant your products in the right hands, and let your customers and partners become your growth engine.

Passive products build trust. AI makes them scalable. Communities make them sticky. Viral loops make them unstoppable.

Your journey doesn't end with publishing a book, launching a course, or uploading a design—it begins there. Every product you release is both an income stream and a signal of authority. By aligning AI-driven tools with human trust and smart distribution, you can create not just revenue, but a self-sustaining ecosystem of assets that earn while you sleep.

And that's the ultimate promise of this new era: **AI doesn't just help you make more—it helps you build something that lasts.**

Glossary of Key Terms

This glossary serves as a quick reference for the most important concepts, tools, and strategies discussed throughout the book. Use it as a companion when revisiting sections or implementing tactics in your own passive income journey.

A

AI (Artificial Intelligence) – Computer systems designed to perform tasks that normally require human intelligence, such as language processing, image recognition, and decision-making.

AI Tutor – An interactive, AI-powered learning assistant that delivers personalized, bite-sized lessons and feedback.

API (Application Programming Interface) – A structured way for different software applications to communicate and work together, often used to automate workflows.

Automation Stack – A collection of tools and integrations that work together to handle repetitive tasks automatically, often including platforms like Zapier, Make, or custom scripts.

B

Blog Cluster – A group of interlinked blog posts organized around a central pillar topic, designed to build topical authority and improve SEO rankings.

Book Funnel – A system where a book serves as the entry point to upsell readers into higher-value products like courses, memberships, or consulting.

C

Chatbot – An AI-powered virtual assistant that provides automated customer support, answers FAQs, or guides buyers through sales funnels.

Clarity Call – A short, paid consulting session designed to provide immediate answers or strategy, often used as an entry-level upsell.

Content Pillars – Core themes or topics that anchor your content strategy and ensure consistency across blogs, newsletters, and social media.

Course Outline – A structured breakdown of modules and lessons used to organize online course material before production.

D

Dynamic Creative Optimization (DCO) – An AI-driven advertising technique where ad text, visuals, and calls-to-action automatically adapt to each viewer.

Dropshipping – An ecommerce model where products are sold through an online store without holding inventory; items are shipped directly from suppliers to customers.

E

Ebook – A digital version of a book, typically in formats like PDF, EPUB, or Kindle-ready files.

Email Funnel – A sequence of automated emails designed to nurture leads, build trust, and drive conversions.

Evergreen Content – Content that remains relevant and continues to generate traffic, leads, or sales over a long period.

F

FAQ Bot – A chatbot configured to answer frequently asked questions using preloaded information or AI.

Freemium Model – A business model where basic products are free, but premium features or access are paid.

G

Gamification – The use of game-like elements such as badges, streaks, or rewards to increase user engagement in courses, apps, or communities.

Google Performance Max – Google's AI-driven ad campaign type that optimizes across all its properties (Search, YouTube, Display, etc.).

I

Influencer Seeding – The strategy of giving products to influencers or community leaders to spark authentic exposure and recommendations.

Interactive Workbook – A structured resource, often AI-enhanced, that guides learners through exercises or reflection prompts.

Internal Linking – The practice of linking between related posts or pages within your site to boost SEO and user navigation.

K

KDP (Kindle Direct Publishing) – Amazon's platform for self-publishing ebooks and print-on-demand paperbacks.

Keyword Research – The process of identifying search terms that potential customers use, guiding content creation and SEO strategy.

M

Membership Community – A recurring revenue model where members pay for access to exclusive content, community, or coaching.

Micro-Learning – Short, focused lessons designed for quick consumption and application.

Monetization Stack – The combination of revenue streams (books, courses, templates, memberships, consulting) that form an author or creator's income ecosystem.

N

Niche Store – A focused ecommerce shop serving a narrow audience or product category, usually with higher authority and conversions than general stores.

No-Code Tools – Platforms that allow non-technical founders to build apps, automations, or websites without writing code.

P

Passive Income – Earnings generated with minimal ongoing effort after an initial setup, such as royalties, subscriptions, or automated sales.

Pillar Post – A long, comprehensive article designed to serve as the foundation of a blog cluster.

POD (Print-on-Demand) – A model where products like books, shirts, or mugs are printed only after a customer orders, eliminating inventory.

R

Referral Loop – A viral mechanic where existing customers are incentivized to invite new users, creating a cycle of growth.

Retargeting Ads – Online ads shown specifically to people who have already visited your site or interacted with your brand.

S

SEO (Search Engine Optimization) – The practice of optimizing content so it ranks higher in search engine results.

Social Auto-Content Engine – A system that automatically creates, repurposes, and schedules social media content at scale.

Substack – A newsletter publishing and monetization platform with built-in subscription tools.

T

Template Pack – A bundle of pre-designed files (for Canva, Notion, Figma, etc.) sold as digital products.

Transactional Bot – A chatbot that executes specific tasks such as order tracking, bookings, or payments.

U

Upsell – A higher-priced offer presented to customers after they purchase a lower-ticket product, often in the form of consulting, advanced courses, or bundles.

User-Generated Content (UGC) – Content created by customers (reviews, photos, testimonials) that can be repurposed for marketing.

V

Viral Loop – A self-perpetuating growth mechanism where each new customer naturally drives new sign-ups or sales.

Voice Synthesis – AI technology that generates lifelike narration, often used in audiobooks or apps.

W

Workflow Automation – A series of automated tasks executed by software tools to reduce manual work, often managed by Zapier or Make.

Work-for-Hire Trap – The cycle of exchanging time directly for money (freelancing or hourly consulting), contrasted with building passive income assets.

Thank You

Thank you for investing your time and attention into this book. I hope the ideas, strategies, and tools you discovered here help you build not just new income streams, but lasting confidence in your ability to create assets that work for you.

A short review on Amazon not only helps other readers decide if this book is right for them — it also ensures that resources like this continue reaching the people who need them most.

Your voice makes a difference. Thank you for being part of this journey.

Eric LeBouthillier

AcraSolution